THE
Compassionate
GOURMET

Contains a wide range of delicious and healthy recipes
reflecting a new approach to vegan cuisine that not only avoids
the suffering and exploitation of animals but is always simply
elegant and often sumptuous.

THE
Compassionate
GOURMET
The Very Best of International Vegan Cuisine
—Janet Hunt—

THORSONS PUBLISHING GROUP
Wellingborough ∗ New York

Published in the UK by Thorsons Publishing Group, Denington Estate,
Wellingborough, Northamptonshire NN8 2RQ, and in the USA by
Thorsons Publishers Inc., 377 Park Avenue South,
New York, NY 10016.
Thorsons Publishers Inc. are distributed to the trade by
Inner Traditions International Ltd., New York.

First published 1986

© JANET HUNT 1986

British Library Cataloguing in Publication Data

Hunt, Janet
The compassionate gourmet: The very best of
international vegan cuisine.
1. Vegetarian cookery
I. Title
641.5'636   TX837

ISBN 0-7225-1155-8)

Library of Congress Cataloging-in-Publication Data

Hunt, Janet.
The compassionate gourmet.

Includes index.
1. Vegetarian cookery.   I.   Title.
TX837.H825 1986   641.5'636   86-1420
ISBN 0-7225-1155-8 (pbk.)

Printed and Bound in Great Britain by
Whitstable Litho Ltd., Whitstable, Kent

CONTENTS

INTRODUCTION

This is a cookbook for animal lovers.

Not the cat-dog-horse set whose double standards allow them to campaign vociferously against cruelty to dumb creatures then go home and tuck into a baby lamb for lunch. Nor those who claim to be so upset by tales of factory-farm and slaughterhouse that they refuse to listen, putting such horrors right out of their minds. They console themselves with the belief that since there are laws about such places, things can't really be that bad. And in any case, they add, they really hardly eat meat at all these days.

This is a cookbook for those who love animals enough to make a conscious decision to stop eating them. And it isn't just meat such people avoid; they accept the misery involved in the production of items such as eggs, milk, gelatine, honey and refuse these too.

Such people are called vegans. They are growing in numbers and strength, and the reasons are many. They have logic as well as compassion on their side: in a world where starvation is rife, is it logical to feed valuable plant proteins to factory-farmed animals in order to get back less food than you started with? Increasingly often they have the medical profession on their side, with more and more of the Western World's ailments being blamed on the saturated fats found in meat and dairy produce. They have ecologists on their side, as concern grows for the world's rain forests, vast expanses of which are being destroyed to provide grazing for meat-producing animals.

If it seems hard to understand why everyone isn't vegan, the answer may well be the vegan diet. Most certainly it is healthy, with its low-fat high-fibre content, inexpensive too. But in general, it isn't exciting. Certainly you can live on nut rissoles, bean loaves and brown rice—but how many people really want to?

7

We no longer eat just to stay alive. We eat to socialize, to celebrate special occasions, to cheer ourselves up. We cook to show our love, to welcome guests, to be creative in the kitchen. Whether this emphasis on food is right or wrong is another question. What IS wrong is that many people who would like to become vegan are failing to do so simply because they are unwilling to give up the pleasures of cooking and eating good foods. And what is sad is that they needn't necessarily do so.

This book aims to show that vegan food can be fit for gourmets. The recipes in it vary from the simple to the sumptuous; dishes that take no time to prepare, others that require speciality ingredients to start with, time and patience to follow, and to finish—an appreciative audience to cheer you to the table! (It does NOT include recipes for nut rissoles or bean loaves.) Hopefully it will encourage more lovers of good food to try a compassionate way of eating, even if only occasionally. As interest grows not just in the philosophy but the food, then undoubtedly veganism will gain the acceptance it deserves. No longer will it be a faddish way of eating for a minority group, a form of self-discipline, self-denial. It may even become fun. And what better way to encourage others to join in?

INGREDIENTS

The interest in natural foods is growing rapidly and with good reason. It makes sense from every point of view to eat more vegetables and fruits, preferably grown without the use of chemicals; to use wholemeal rather than white bread; to get your protein from nuts and beans and whole grains. Not everyone, however, has access to the best quality foods. Not all vegans (despite the traditional view of such people) live in the country, grow their own produce, grind their own flour. Many city dwellers are more sensitive and concerned about animals than those who actually live surrounded by nature; and many vegans not only live in cities, but work there too, which means the time they have to shop and prepare food may well be limited.

There is a place for convenience foods in a healthy diet, provided they are used as extras and not as basics. Many such ingredients can save time when you are short of it, can add zip to a simple dish, can help you work a miracle when the cupboard is almost bare. It is not always easy to know which products are OK for vegans and which are taboo, but reading labels will help. So will writing to manufacturers. And an excellent booklet called *The Vegan Shoppers' Guide* is now being produced (and updated continually)—well worth sending off for a copy.

While experimenting with recipes for this book I used many products, some of which worked better than others. Listed below are just a few of the ingredients sold in the U.K. that worked best for me. (If you live outside the U.K., check with your local health food store for comparable products.)

BILLINGTON'S RAW CANE SUGAR

BURGESS SWEET 'N' SOUR SAUCE. A quick and easy substitute for the real one on page 70. They also make a tasty BARBECUE SAUCE.

CAULDRON FOODS plain and smoked tofu.

* DIRECT FOODS PROTOVEG soya "meat."

INFINITY FOODS (Distributors). Soya mayonnaise.

JUS-ROL ALL VEGETABLE PUFF PASTRY. Make vol-au-vents in minutes.

* LOTUS FOODS TVP. Soya "meats" in a variety of forms and flavours.

McCORMICKS BACON FLAVOUR SALAD TOPPING. Due to be reintroduced shortly under the SCHWARTZ SPICES label, with their assurance it will still be suitable for vegans.

MITCHELHILL DIGESTIVE BISCUITS

PLAMIL CONCENTRATED SOYA MILK. Used diluted as a milk, undiluted as a cream.

RAYNERS NATURAL VANILLA ESSENCE

SAINSBURY'S JAMS

TERRY'S BITTER CHOCOLATE

TOMOR MARGARINE. There are now a wide variety of vegan margarines available, most of them very good. I still prefer this old favourite when cooking.

* Many people within the vegetarian and vegan movement are against the use of these soya "meats," even though they contain no animal ingredients. Personally I have no idea if they taste like the real thing, nor am I bothered. When served up in sauces I find them delicious, satisfying, and—so the manufacturers inform us—am eating a nutritionally sound food. That is enough for me. Those who wish to avoid them can adapt recipes that include soya "meats" by adding beans, lentils or vegetables to the recipe in their place.

9

One other ingredient you will find dotted through the following pages is alcohol. Again I feel this is an ingredient that makes the food more interesting, hence my decision to use it. In cooked dishes, of course, the alcohol content evaporates to leave a slight taste only, so those that fear becoming alcoholic need not worry. A more real worry may be that some alcohols are produced by methods that involve animal products; many, however, are not. Finding out which alcohols are acceptable is not easy, and in any case, methods may change within individual companies, so it must be hard if not impossible to ever be certain. The choice is yours.

How to be Vegan

As this is a cookbook and not a book about health (though hopefully you will become healthier by following the recipes and eating the vegan way!), this is not the place to go into the nutritional aspects of a vegan diet. If you have only just decided to make the change and need sound advice on how to balance your diet, and for copies of The Vegan Shoppers' Guide, contact: The Vegan Society, 33/35 George Street, Oxford OX1 2AY, England.

BREAKFASTS

TROPICAL MUESLI

Imperial (Metric)	American
1 lb (455g) rolled oats	4 cups rolled oats
4 oz (115g) flaked coconut	1 ⅓ cups flaked coconut
4 oz (115g) banana chips	4 ounces banana chips
4 oz (115g) Brazil nut pieces	¾ cup Brazil nut pieces
4 oz (115g) candied pineapple	4 ounces candied pineapple
2 oz (55g) bran	1 cup bran
1–2 teaspoons mixed spice, or to taste	1–2 teaspoons mixed spice, or to taste

1. Simply mix together all the ingredients, making sure they are evenly distributed.

2. Store in a large screwtop jar and use as needed.

3. Serve this muesli with diluted fruit juice (pineapple is delicious) or with soya milk.

NOTE: The flaked coconut can be lightly roasted first to give extra flavour. Most banana chips are sweetened with white sugar, but some contain honey—check when you buy them. (You could, of course, use chopped dried banana instead, or even add fresh banana as you serve the muesli.)

BLACKBERRY MUESLI

Imperial (Metric)
4 oz (115g) mixed cereal base
4 oz (115g) mixed chopped nuts
2 tablespoons lemon juice
water or apple juice to mix
1 large apple
approximately 6 oz (170g) fresh blackberries
maple syrup or raw cane sugar to sweeten (optional)

American
1 cup mixed cereal base
¾ cup mixed chopped nuts
2 tablespoons lemon juice
water or apple juice to mix
1 large apple
1½ cups fresh blackberries
maple syrup or raw cane sugar to sweeten (optional)

1. In a bowl, mix together the cereal base and most of the chopped nuts then stir in the lemon juice. Add enough water or diluted apple juice to moisten well. Cover and leave overnight.

2. Grate the unpeeled apple and add to the muesli; wash and add the blackberries. Adjust liquid if necessary.

3. Divide into 4 bowls. Sprinkle with the remaining nuts. If the fruit is ripe, this muesli should be sweet enough, but if not add maple syrup or sugar to taste. Serve at once.

FRUIT AND SUNFLOWER MUESLI

Imperial (Metric)	American
¾ lb (340g) mixed cereal base	3 cups mixed cereal base
3 oz (85g) raisins	½ cup raisins
3 oz (85g) dried apricot pieces	½ cup dried apricot pieces
4 oz (115g) sunflower seeds	1 scant cup sunflower seeds
2 oz (55g) pumpkin seeds	½ cup pumpkin seeds
2 oz (55g) toasted wheatgerm	½ cup toasted wheatgerm

1. Put the cereal base into a bowl and stir in the raisins.

2. Chop the dried apricots. Add to the first mixture together with the sunflower and pumpkin seeds. Stir in the wheatgerm.

3. Store in a large screwtop jar and use as needed. Undiluted soya milk makes a creamy special-occasion topping.

Walnut Maple Granola

Imperial (Metric)	American
1 lb (455g) mixed cereal base	4 cups mixed cereal base
2 oz (55g) wheatgerm	½ cup wheatgerm
2 oz (55g) sesame seeds	½ cup sesame seeds
4 oz (115g) walnut pieces	¾ cup walnut pieces
2 oz (55g) desiccated coconut	⅔ cup desiccated coconut
⅛ pint (70ml) water	¼ cup water
⅛ pint (70ml) vegetable oil	¼ cup vegetable oil
½ teaspoon natural vanilla essence	½ teaspoon natural vanilla extract
4 tablespoons maple or golden syrup	4 tablespoons maple syrup
4 oz (115g) dates, chopped	⅔ cup dates, chopped

1. Mix together the cereal base, wheatgerm, sesame seeds, walnut pieces and coconut.

2. Stir together the water, vegetable oil, vanilla and maple syrup.

3. Moisten the dry ingredients with the water mixture, mixing them thoroughly. Spread evenly across the base of a large, lightly greased baking tray.

4. Bake at 375°F/190°C (Gas Mark 5) about 30 minutes, stirring every 10 minutes. When the mixture is beginning to crisp, add the chopped dates. Cook until golden.

5. Leave to cool on the baking tray. When completely cold, transfer to a large screwtop jar.

6. Serve as needed, moistening with a little soya milk.

MALTED OAT CRUNCH WITH PEARS

Imperial (Metric)	American
¾ lb (340g) rolled oats	3 cups rolled oats
1 oz (30g) soya flour	¼ cup soy flour
4 oz (115g) coarsely chopped mixed nuts	¾ cup coarsely chopped mixed nuts
4 tablespoons vegetable oil	4 tablespoons vegetable oil
4 tablespoons malt extract	4 tablespoons malt extract
2 tablespoons grated orange peel	2 tablespoons grated orange peel
4 oz (115g) dried pears	1 scant cup dried pears

1. Mix together the oats, flour and nuts.

2. In a large, heavy-based pan gently heat the oil and malt extract. Add the orange peel.

3. Stir in the oat mixture, making sure all the ingredients are coated with oil and malt (use a little more if necessary).

4. Heat gently, stirring frequently, until the oats are golden and crunchy. Remove the pan from the heat.

5. Chop the pears and stir them into the warm oat mixture. Leave to get completely cold before storing in a large screwtop jar.

6. Serve with soya milk.

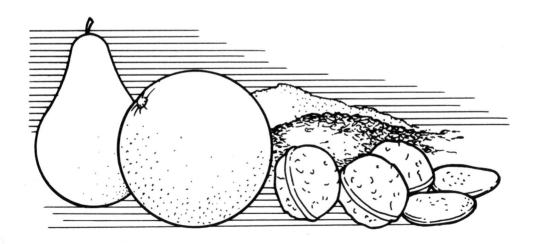

Cinnamon Prunes and Grapefruit

Imperial (Metric)	American
½ lb (225g) prunes	2 scant cups prunes
1 lemon	1 lemon
1 teaspoon ground cinnamon or to taste	1 teaspoon ground cinnamon or to taste
1 grapefruit	1 grapefruit

1. Wash the prunes well. Put them into a saucepan and just cover with water. Add the juice of the lemon, 2 tablespoons of finely chopped lemon peel and the cinnamon.

2. Bring to a boil then cover the pan and simmer gently until the prunes are soft. Remove the lid and continue cooking over medium heat until most of the liquid has evaporated.

3. Spoon the warm or chilled prunes into 4 small bowls. Divide the peeled grapefruit into segments and stir them in with the prunes or arrange them decoratively around the edge of the bowls.

NOTE: To make this into a complete breakfast dish, sprinkle it with nuts, granola or muesli. Vegan yogurt also can be added for extra protein.

Hot Wheatgerm Breakfast

Imperial (Metric)	American
4 oz (115g) wheatgerm	1 cup wheatgerm
2 oz (55g) rolled oats	½ cup rolled oats
approximately ½ pint (285ml) water	1⅓ cups water
2 oz (55g) raisins	⅓ cup raisins
1 oz (30g) coarsely chopped almonds	3 tablespoons coarsely chopped almonds
raw cane sugar to taste (optional)	raw cane sugar to taste (optional)
soya milk	soy milk
fresh or stewed fruit (optional)	fresh or stewed fruit (optional)

1. Mix the wheatgerm and oats and put them into a saucepan with the water.

2. Stir well, bring gently to a boil, then simmer the mixture a few minutes.

3. Remove from the heat and add the raisins, nuts and sugar to taste.

4. Divide among 4 warmed bowls and serve at once topped with a little soya milk.

5. Fresh fruit can be added if liked. Stewed fruit also goes well—if it has been sweetened, you will probably not need to add any sugar to the wheatgerm.

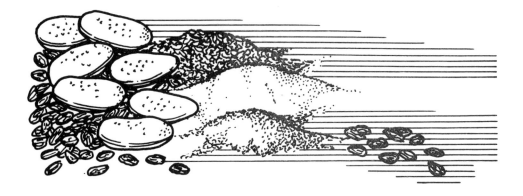

CASHEW TOAST

Imperial (Metric)	American
2 oz (55g) cashews	½ cup cashews
⅓ pint (200ml) soya milk	¾ cup soy milk
seasoning to taste	seasoning to taste
6 slices wholemeal bread	6 slices whole wheat bread
approximately 1 oz (30g) vegan margarine	2½ tablespoons vegan margarine
2 bananas	2 bananas
maple syrup or raw cane sugar	maple syrup or raw cane sugar

1. Grind the nuts to a powder then whisk them with the milk. Season generously.

2. Pour into a shallow bowl. Cut the bread in triangles. Dip each piece of bread into the mixture, making sure they are all evenly coated.

3. Melt a little margarine in a frying pan. Sauté the bread slices just a few minutes until lightly browned. Turn and cook the other side.

4. Keep cooked slices warm while cooking any remaining bread in the same way, adding more margarine as necessary.

5. Serve 3 pieces to each person, topping them with sliced banana. Hand round syrup or sugar at the table.

KEDGEREE

Imperial (Metric)	American
½lb (225g) smoked tofu	1 cup smoked tofu
1 pint (570ml) water	2½ cups water
6 oz (170g) brown long-grain rice	¾cup brown long-grain rice
1 large onion	1 large onion
approximately 3 tablespoons vegetable oil	approximately 3 tablespoons vegetable oil
seasoning to taste	seasoning to taste
cayenne pepper	cayenne pepper
chopped parsley	chopped parsley

1. Drain and coarsely chop the tofu then set aside.

2. Bring the water to a boil and add the rice. Lower the heat, and simmer, covered, about 30 minutes or until the rice is just cooked. Drain if necessary.

3. Meanwhile slice the onion. Heat the oil and sauté the onion until it begins to soften. Add the tofu and cook just long enough for it to heat through, stirring occasionally as necessary.

4. Mix together the rice and onion and tofu mixture, adding any of the oil left in the pan. Flavour well with seasoning and cayenne pepper.

5. Transfer to a warmed serving dish and sprinkle generously with chopped parsley.

FRUIT AND NUT BREAKFAST DRINK

Imperial (Metric)
6 oz (170g) dried apricot pieces
4 oz (115g) almonds
⅛ pint (70ml) lemon juice
¼ pint (140ml) frozen orange juice
concentrate (defrosted)
½ teaspoon natural almond extract
crushed ice cubes (optional)
water
fresh mint to garnish

American
1 cup dried apricot pieces
1 cup almonds
¼ cup lemon juice
⅔ cup frozen orange juice
concentrate (defrosted)
½ teaspoon natural almond extract
crushed ice cubes (optional)
water
fresh mint to garnish

1. Wash the apricots then cover them with boiling water and leave to soak overnight. (If very hard, they may need to be lightly cooked to soften).

2. In a blender, whirl together the drained apricot pieces, almonds, lemon juice, orange juice, almond extract and ice cubes, if using them (and if your blender will take them).

3. Dilute the mixture to taste with water. Pour into 3 or 4 tall glasses, garnish with mint and serve at once.

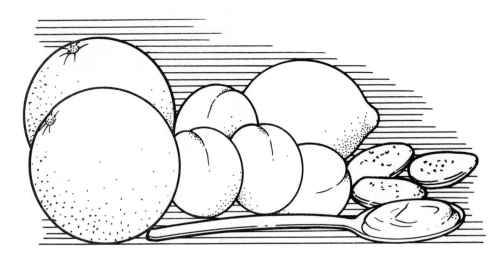

Orange Marmalade with Whisky

Imperial (Metric)	American
1 lb (455g) Seville oranges	1 pound Seville oranges
juice of 1 large lemon	juice of 1 large lemon
3 pints (1.7l) water	3 pints water
3 lb (1.7kg) raw cane sugar	3 pounds raw cane sugar
⅛ pint (70ml) whisky	¼ cup Scotch whisky

1. Scrub the oranges, cut them into halves and squeeze well to remove the juice and seeds.

2. Chop or mince the peel. Tie the seeds in a muslin (cheesecloth) bag.

3. Put the peel, orange and lemon juice, water and bag of seeds into a large saucepan or preserving pan. Bring to a boil, lower the heat and simmer 1–2 hours, or until volume is reduced by about one third.

4. Lift out the bag, and when cool enough to handle, squeeze to release any trapped liquid. Discard the bag.

5. Use a wooden spoon to stir in the sugar and heat gently, stirring continually, until it dissolves. Add the whisky.

6. Bring the mixture to a boil and cook rapidly 10–15 minutes or until setting point (see note) is reached. Allow to cool in the pan 5–10 minutes.

7. When the marmalade begins to stiffen, stir to distribute the peel. Pour into dry, warmed, sterilized jars and top with waxed paper rounds. When cold, seal the jars. Store in a cool, dark place.

Makes 4–5 lbs (1.8–2.2kg).

NOTE: To test if marmalade has reached setting point spoon a little onto a cold saucer and leave 1 minute. Push it gently; if it wrinkles, it is ready. Test frequently as marmalade can be ruined if cooked either too short or too long a time.

WHOLE STRAWBERRY JAM

Imperial (Metric)	American
2 lbs (900g) strawberries	2 pounds strawberries
2 lbs (900g) raw cane sugar	4 cups raw cane sugar
3 lemons	3 lemons

1. Check that the strawberries are firm and even sized. Wash and hull them, then layer in a large bowl, sprinkling each layer generously with sugar. Leave overnight or even longer (24 hours is ideal).

2. Transfer the strawberries and sugar to a large saucepan or preserving pan. Halve and squeeze the lemons, adding the juice to the pan. Tie the pith and seeds in a muslin (cheesecloth) bag and add this also.

3. Boil the mixture gently about 1 hour or until setting point is reached. (See Orange Marmalade with Whisky for testing method.) The jam will need to be stirred frequently to prevent sticking, but try not to break up the strawberries.

4. Discard the seeds and allow the jam to cool slightly. Pour into dry, warmed, sterilized jars and cover with rounds of waxed paper. When cold, seal the jars. Store in a cool, dark place.

Makes approximately 3 lbs (1.4kg)

NOTE: Sprinkling the strawberries with sugar and leaving them overnight strengthens the skins so that the strawberries are less inclined to break up. Although less attractive to look at, strawberry jam can also be made from crushed strawberries, in which case Step 1 can be omitted.

Soups, Pâtés and Other Starters

Soups

Mulligatawny Soup

Imperial (Metric)	American
2 medium carrots	2 medium carrots
1 large potato	1 large potato
1 large onion	1 large onion
1 green pepper	1 green pepper
1 cooking apple	1 cooking apple
2 tablespoons vegetable oil	2 tablespoons vegetable oil
½ oz (15g) wholemeal flour	2 tablespoons whole wheat flour
2 teaspoons curry powder	2 teaspoons curry powder
2 oz (55g) sultanas	⅓ cup golden seedless raisins
1½ pints (850ml) water	3¾ cups water
2 oz (55g) split red lentils	⅓ cup split red lentils
seasoning to taste	seasoning to taste

1. Scrub the vegetables and apple; peel if necessary. Dice into even sized pieces (reserve a little of the pepper for a garnish).

2. Heat the oil in a large pan and sauté the prepared vegetables a few minutes, stirring occasionally.

3. Mix together the flour and curry powder. Add to the pan, stir, and cook a minute or two more.

4. Add the sultanas (seedless raisins), the water and lentils. Bring to a boil, then cover the pan and simmer about 30 minutes or until all the ingredients are cooked.

5. Liquidize in a blender. Add a drop more stock or water if necessary. Return the mixture to the saucepan and reheat gently. Divide the soup among 4 bowls and garnish with the remaining pepper, cut into very fine strips.

Pumpkin Soup

Imperial (Metric)	American
2 tablespoons vegetable oil	2 tablespoons vegetable oil
1 small onion, finely chopped	1 small onion, finely chopped
1½ lbs (680g) fresh pumpkin, peeled and cubed	1½ pounds fresh pumpkin, peeled and cubed
1½ pints (850ml) vegetable stock	3¾ cups vegetable stock
generous pinch raw cane sugar	generous pinch raw cane sugar
generous pinch ground cloves	generous pinch ground cloves
½ pint (385ml) soya milk	1⅓ cup soy milk
seasoning to taste	seasoning to taste
2 tablespoons dry sherry (optional)	2 tablespoons dry sherry (optional)
2 tablespoons undiluted soya milk	2 tablespoons undiluted soy milk
wholemeal croûtons to garnish (see note)	whole wheat croûtons to garnish (see note)

1. Heat the oil in a large saucepan. Gently sauté the onion until beginning to colour. Add the pumpkin and cook a few minutes more, stirring occasionally.

2. Add the stock, sugar, cloves and soya milk. Bring to a boil then cover; lower heat and simmer 15–20 minutes or until pumpkin is cooked.

3. The ingredients can be put through a blender, but for a more interesting texture press them through a sieve. Reheat gently. Season to taste and add the soya milk. Do not let the soup boil.

4. Serve at once in 4 warmed bowls, sprinkling the tops with golden croûtons.

NOTE: To make the croûtons, cut 2 slices wholemeal bread into cubes and sauté until crisp and brown in 2 tablespoons oil or a mixture of oil and vegan margarine. Drain well.

SPICED LENTIL SOUP WITH ENDIVE (CHICORY)

Imperial (Metric)

½ lb (225g) brown lentils, soaked overnight
1 onion, coarsely chopped
1 ½ pints (850ml) vegetable stock
approximately 6 large outer leaves of endive
2 teaspoons vegetable oil
1 teaspoon ground coriander
½ teaspoon ground cumin
1 clove garlic, crushed
seasoning to taste

American

1 cup brown lentils, soaked overnight
1 onion, coarsely chopped
3 ¾ cups vegetable stock
approximately 6 large outer leaves of chicory
2 teaspoons vegetable oil
1 teaspoon ground coriander
½ teaspoon ground cumin
1 clove garlic, crushed
seasoning to taste

1. Drain the lentils and put them into a saucepan with the onion and the vegetable stock. Bring to a boil, then simmer 20–30 minutes or until almost soft.

2. Wash and shred the endive (chicory) leaves and add to the lentils. Cook 10 minutes more or until both lentils and endive (chicory) are tender.

3. Meanwhile heat the oil in a small, clean saucepan and add the spices and garlic. Cook gently 5–10 minutes. Stir the mixture into the contents of the first pan and season to taste.

RED PEPPER SOUP

Imperial (Metric)	American
1 small cauliflower	1 small cauliflower
2 small red peppers	2 small red peppers
1 onion	1 onion
7 oz (200g) tin tomatoes	small can tomatoes
2 inch (5 cm) piece of cucumber, peeled	2 inch piece of cucumber, peeled
1½ pints (850ml) vegetable stock	3¾ cups vegetable stock
pinch dry mustard	pinch dry mustard
seasoning to taste	seasoning to taste
beansprouts to garnish	beansprouts to garnish

1. Trim and coarsely chop the cauliflower. Slice the pepper and onion. Coarsely chop the tomatoes and cucumber.

2. Combine all the ingredients in a saucepan and bring to a boil. Cover the pan and simmer 15–20 minutes or until everything is cooked but still crisp.

3. If liked you can liquidize the soup to make it smooth, in which case you will need to reheat gently.

4. Adjust seasoning and garnish with a sprinkling of beansprouts.

BEAN AND SWEETCORN CHOWDER

Imperial (Metric)	American
1 oz (30g) vegan margarine	2½ tablespoons vegan margarine
½ oz (15g) wholemeal flour	2 tablespoons whole wheat flour
1¾ pints (1 litre) vegetable stock	4½ cups vegetable stock
½ lb (225g) green beans, fresh or frozen	8 ounces green beans, fresh or frozen
4 oz (115g) sweetcorn, fresh or frozen	⅔ cup corn, fresh or frozen
2 oz (55g) bulgur	⅓ cup bulgur
approximately ½ tablespoon marjoram	approximately ½ tablespoon marjoram
seasoning to taste	seasoning to taste
soya sauce	soy sauce
½ oz (15g) flaked almonds, roasted	2 tablespoons slivered almonds, roasted

1. Melt the margarine in a saucepan, stir in the flour and cook a few minutes.

2. Add the stock, stir well and bring the mixture to a boil. Add the beans, corn, bulgur and marjoram.

3. Lower the heat and simmer 10–20 minutes or until vegetables are just cooked. Season and flavour with soya sauce to taste.

4. Garnish each of 4 bowls of the soup with a sprinkling of almonds.

CREAM OF PARSNIP SOUP

Imperial (Metric)	American
2 tablespoons vegetable oil	2 tablespoons vegetable oil
1 large carrot	1 large carrot
1 medium onion	1 medium onion
2 medium parsnips	2 medium parsnips
1½ pints (850ml) vegetable stock or water	3¾ cups vegetable stock or water
½ teaspoon basil or to taste	½ teaspoon basil or to taste
seasoning to taste	seasoning to taste
3–4 tablespoons hummus (see page 76)	3–4 tablespoons hummus (see page 76)
chopped fresh basil or parsley to garnish	chopped fresh basil or parsley to garnish

1. Heat the oil in a large pan. Peel and coarsely chop the carrot, onion and parsnips and add to the pan. Sauté gently, stirring occasionally, until they begin to colour.

2. Add the vegetable stock and basil, bring to a boil then cover and simmer 20 minutes or until all the ingredients are cooked.

3. Season the soup to taste. Stir in the hummus so that it melts to make the texture thick and creamy. Heat a minute longer.

4. Divide between 4 bowls and garnish, if possible, with fresh basil leaves. Serve at once.

NOTE: This is an ideal soup when you have some leftover hummus you want to use up. You can, if you prefer, add a few spoonfuls of tahini to give the soup a creamy texture.

Green Vichyssoise

Imperial (Metric)	American
2 small bunches watercress	2 small bunches watercress
1 oz (30g) vegan margarine	2½ tablespoons vegan margarine
1 small onion	1 small onion
1¼ pints (710ml) vegetable stock	3 cups vegetable stock
seasoning to taste	seasoning to taste
¾ lb (340g) potatoes	¾ pound potatoes
½ pint (285ml) soya milk	1⅓ cups soy milk
approximately ⅛ pint (70ml) undiluted soya milk	approximately ¼ cup undiluted soy milk

1. Wash and trim most of the watercress. Reserve a spoonful of the leaves.

2. Melt the margarine in a saucepan and sauté the chopped onion 5 minutes or until it begins to soften.

3. Add the stock and seasoning; peel and dice the potatoes and add to the pan; cover and simmer 10 minutes to cook the potatoes.

4. Add the prepared watercress, bring to a boil then remove at once. Stir in the soya milk. Purée the contents of the pan in a blender.

5. Cool and then chill the soup. Divide between 4 bowls. Just before serving stir in a few spoonsful of undiluted soya milk. Garnish with the extra watercress leaves.

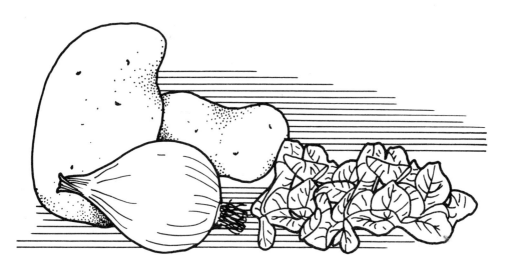

CHILLED PEANUT SOUP

Imperial (Metric)	*American*
2 tablespoons vegetable oil	2 tablespoons vegetable oil
1 carrot, finely chopped	1 carrot, finely chopped
1 stick celery, finely chopped	1 stalk celery, finely chopped
1 small onion, finely chopped	1 small onion, finely chopped
1 teaspoon curry powder	1 teaspoon curry powder
1 oz (30g) wholemeal flour	¼ cup whole wheat flour
1 pint (570ml) vegetable stock	2½ cups vegetable stock
½ pint (285ml) soya milk	1⅓ cups soy milk
2 oz (55g) peanut butter	½ cup peanut butter
seasoning to taste	seasoning to taste
paprika and celery leaves to garnish	paprika and celery leaves to garnish

1. Heat the oil in a large pan, then sauté the carrot, celery and onion 5 minutes or until beginning to soften.

2. Sprinkle in the curry powder and cook briefly; add the flour and cook a few minutes more.

3. Stir in the vegetable stock and milk and bring to a boil. Cover the pan and simmer the vegetables 10 minutes.

4. The soup can be left as it is, or blended for a smoother texture. Stir in the peanut butter, making sure it dissolves completely, and season to taste.

5. Leave to cool, then chill the soup. Pour into 4 bowls and garnish with paprika for colour plus a sprinkling of chopped celery leaves.

Pâtés

Avocado Tofu Pâté

Imperial (Metric)	American
2 ripe avocados	2 ripe avocados
squeeze of lemon juice	squeeze of lemon juice
5 oz (140g) tofu	⅔ cup tofu
1–2 spring onions	1–2 scallions
½ clove garlic (optional)	½ clove garlic (optional)
seasoning to taste	seasoning to taste
watercress to garnish	watercress to garnish

1. Peel the avocados and remove their stones. Mash the flesh with the lemon juice.

2. Drain the tofu and mash well, then stir in the avocado.

3. Very finely chop the spring onions (scallions) and garlic. Add to the first mixture. Season to taste.

4. Transfer to a small serving dish, cover and chill well. Serve garnished with sprigs of watercress.

CURRIED HAZELNUT PÂTÉ

Imperial (Metric)	*American*
4 oz (115g) hazelnuts	**¾ cup hazelnuts**
approximately 4 tablespoons	**approximately 4 tablespoons**
vegetable oil	**vegetable oil**
½ small onion, finely chopped	**½ small onion, finely chopped**
2 teaspoons curry powder or to	**2 teaspoons curry powder or to**
taste	**taste**
lemon twists to garnish	**lemon twists to garnish**

1. Grind the hazelnuts to a fine powder.

2. Heat the oil in a saucepan and add the onion. Cook until it begins to colour. Stir in the curry powder and cook a minute or two more.

3. Remove the pan from the heat and stir in the hazelnuts, mixing thoroughly. Add a drop more oil if the mixture seems too dry.

4. Transfer to a small dish, smooth the top and set aside to cool. Cover and chill briefly before serving. Top with twists of lemon.

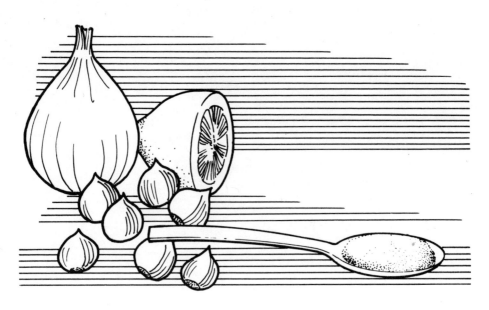

SPINACH PÂTÉ

Imperial (Metric)	American
2 lbs (1.15 kilos) spinach	2 pounds spinach
1 oz (30g) vegan margarine	2½ tablespoons vegan margarine
½ small onion, chopped	½ small onion, chopped
⅛ pint (70ml) soya milk	¼ cup soy milk
generous pinch nutmeg	generous pinch nutmeg
seasoning to taste	seasoning to taste
approximately 2 oz (55g) fine wholemeal breadcrumbs	1 cup fine whole wheat breadcrumbs
½ oz (15g) peanuts, coarsely crushed	2 tablespoons peanuts, coarsely crushed

1. Wash the spinach and drop into boiling water. Cook a few minutes only then drain very well. When cool enough to handle chop the spinach as finely as possible.

2. Melt the margarine in a saucepan and add the onion, sautéing it gently until it begins to colour. Mix in the spinach and cook 5 minutes more.

3. Add the soya milk and cook gently until this is absorbed by the spinach. Stir in the nutmeg and seasoning.

4. Off the heat add enough breadcrumbs to thicken the mixture to a pâté consistency. Transfer to a small serving dish, smooth the top, sprinkle with the peanuts.

5. Cover and chill well before serving.

NOTE: When fresh spinach is not available the frozen variety could be used. In that case omit Step 1. Simply defrost the spinach then drain well.

Sunflower and Pepper Pâté

Imperial (Metric)	American
5 oz (140g) sunflower seeds	1 cup sunflower seeds
2 oz (55g) vegan margarine	¼ cup vegan margarine
½ red pepper, finely chopped	½ red pepper, finely chopped
pinch garlic salt	pinch garlic salt
fresh ground pepper	fresh ground pepper
½ teaspoon oregano or to taste	½ teaspoon oregano or to taste
extra seeds and red pepper rings to garnish	extra seeds and red pepper rings to garnish

1. Roast the sunflower seeds in a dry pan over low heat, stirring frequently. When they begin to colour set aside to cool.

2. Grind the sunflower seeds to a powder.

3. Soften the margarine, add the seeds, pepper, seasoning and oregano. Make sure all the ingredients are well blended.

4. Spoon into a small serving dish; smooth the top. Cover and chill until needed. Serve decorated with a few extra seeds, and red pepper rings.

AUBERGINE (EGGPLANT) PÂTÉ WITH TAHINI

Imperial (Metric)	American
1 large aubergine	1 large eggplant
1 small clove garlic, crushed	1 small clove garlic, crushed
1 small lemon	1 small lemon
seasoning to taste	seasoning to taste
¼ pint (140ml) olive oil	⅔ cup olive oil
2–3 tablespoons tahini	2–3 tablespoons tahini
a few black olives	a few black olives
fresh chopped parsley to garnish	fresh chopped parsley to garnish

1. Prick the aubergine (eggplant) then either grill it under high heat, turning it frequently, or put it into a medium-hot oven (375°F/190°C—Gas Mark 5) for an hour or so.

2. When the skin is black and the flesh soft, set it aside to cool.

3. Rub the burnt skin off, or halve the aubergine (eggplant) and scoop out all the flesh. Chop this coarsely.

4. Put the flesh in a bowl and add the garlic and the juice from the lemon. Season to taste. Beat well until smooth (or purée in a blender).

5. Gradually mix in the olive oil, making sure it is completely absorbed. Then stir in the tahini to make a thick smooth mixture.

6. Transfer to a serving dish. The olives can be chopped and mixed into the other ingredients or sprinkled on top. Garnish generously with chopped parsley.

CELERY MISO PÂTÉ

Imperial (Metric)
scant ¼ pint (140ml) vegetable
stock
1 tablespoon miso
crumbs from 2 slices wholemeal
bread
½ clove garlic, crushed
2 sticks celery, finely chopped
½ onion, finely chopped
2 oz (55g) walnuts
2 tablespoons parsley
seasoning to taste
celery leaves to garnish

American
scant ⅔ cup vegetable stock
1 tablespoon miso
crumbs from 2 slices whole
wheat bread
½ clove garlic, crushed
2 stalks celery, finely chopped
½ onion, finely chopped
½ cup walnuts
2 tablespoons parsley
seasoning to taste
celery leaves to garnish

1. Mix the warm stock with the miso.

2. Put the liquid into a bowl and stir in the bread. Add the garlic, celery and onion.

3. Coarsely crush and stir in the walnuts, then add the parsley and seasoning. Mix thoroughly.

4. Cover the mixture and leave to stand overnight.

5. Put the pâté in a serving dish and garnish with celery leaves.

OTHER STARTERS

WATERMELON COCKTAIL

Imperial (Metric)	American
½ medium watermelon*	½ medium watermelon*
1 tablespoon lemon juice	1 tablespoon lemon juice
1–2 oz (30–55g) raw cane sugar, powdered in grinder	approximately ⅓ cup raw cane sugar, powdered in grinder
1–2 tablespoons chopped sweet cicely—optional	1–2 tablespoons chopped sweet cicely—optional
fresh mint sprigs to garnish	fresh mint sprigs to garnish

1. Use a small round scoop to shape the melon flesh into balls.

2. Put them into a bowl and carefully stir in the lemon juice, mixing it well. Sprinkle with sugar to sweeten according to taste. Add the finely chopped sweet cicely if using it.

3. Chill the melon balls for at least half an hour.

4. Serve in individual bowls or glasses, topping each one with a sprig or two of fresh mint.

* Any kind of melon can be used in this recipe. For especially interesting visual effects, try combining two or three different varieties.

CREAMY PEA VOL-AU-VENTS

Imperial (Metric)	American
For puff pastry:	*For puff pastry:*
½ lb (225g) wholemeal flour	2 cups whole wheat flour
pinch salt	pinch salt
few drops lemon juice	few drops lemon juice
approximately ¼ pint (140ml) ice-cold water	⅔ cup ice-cold water
7 oz (200g) vegan margarine	generous ⅔ cup vegan margarine
For filling:	*For filling:*
3 oz (85g) cooked peas	½ cup cooked peas
2 firm tomatoes, coarsely chopped	2 firm tomatoes, coarsely chopped
2 tablespoons vegetable oil	2 tablespoons vegetable oil
½ small onion, finely chopped	½ small onion, finely chopped
1 oz (30g) wholemeal flour	¼ cup whole wheat flour
approximately ⅓ pint (200ml) soya milk	¾ cup soy milk
seasoning to taste	seasoning to taste
parsley to garnish	parsley to garnish

1. Sift the flour and set aside the bran to use in another recipe. Sieve the flour and salt into a bowl. Add lemon juice and water to make a dough.

2. On a floured board roll dough out into an oblong. Put the margarine in the centre then fold first the bottom section of pastry then the top, so that the margarine is covered.

3. Turn the dough, seal the edges and use a rolling pin to "rib" the dough at intervals to give a corrugated look.

4. Roll out the pastry, fold the top and then the bottom as before, seal the edges and "rib" again.

5. Turn and repeat. For really light pastry you should do this at least 6 times in all, preferably more. If possible, wrap the pastry in foil and chill 30 minutes between some, if not all, of the rollings to stop it becoming too soft. Chill well before using.

6. Roll out the pastry carefully on a floured board to just under ½ inch (1.25cm) in thickness. Cut into 4 medium sized cases. Bake at 425°F/220°C (Gas Mark 7) 15–20 minutes, or until crisp and golden.

7. Meanwhile drain the peas and mix with the tomatoes.

8. Heat the oil and sauté the onion for a few minutes. Sprinkle in the flour, stir and cook a few minutes more. Add the milk, stir, bring to a boil then simmer to make a thick sauce. Add the milk, stir, bring to a boil then simmer to make a thick sauce. Season.

9. Mix the peas and tomatoes into the sauce.

10. Put one of the hot vol-au-vent cases onto each of 4 small serving plates and fill each one with some of the creamy pea mixture. Garnish with parsley. Serve at once.

Imam Bayeldi (Stuffed Aubergine or Eggplant)

Imperial (Metric)	*American*
4 small aubergines	**4 small eggplants**
1 onion	**1 onion**
2 tablespoons vegetable oil	**2 tablespoons vegetable oil**
7 oz (200g) tin tomatoes	**small can tomatoes**
2 tablespoons currants	**2 tablespoons currants**
pinch cinnamon	**pinch of cinnamon**
seasoning to taste	**seasoning to taste**
2 tablespoons fresh chopped parsley	**2 tablespoons fresh chopped parsley**
1 oz (30g) pine nuts	**3 tablespoons pine nuts**
⅛ pint (70ml) water	**¼ cup water**
⅛ pint (70ml) vegetable oil	**¼ cup vegetable oil**
generous squeeze lemon juice	**generous squeeze lemon juice**
pinch raw cane sugar	**pinch raw cane sugar**
½ clove garlic, crushed	**½ clove garlic, crushed**
1 bayleaf, crushed	**1 bayleaf, crushed**
watercress to garnish	**watercress to garnish**

1. Wash and cut slits in the aubergines (eggplants). Sprinkle with salt and leave 30 minutes. Rinse with cold water, then stand upside down to drain.

2. Chop the onion. Heat the oil and sauté the onion until it begins to soften.

3. Drain and coarsely chop the tomatoes and add with the currants, cinnamon and seasoning. Cook 20–30 minutes to thicken.

4. Stir in the parsley and pine nuts. Use the mixture to stuff the slits in the aubergines.

5. Arrange them side by side in a shallow pan.

6. Mix together the water, oil, lemon juice, sugar, garlic and bayleaf. Pour the liquid over the aubergines.

7. Cover the aubergines with foil. Bake at 350°F/180°C (Gas Mark 4) 30 minutes or until tender.

8. Chill the aubergines. Divide onto 4 small plates and garnish with watercress. Good served with wholemeal toast.

Tomato Ice

Imperial (Metric)	American
1 ½ lbs (680g) tomatoes	1 ½ pounds tomatoes
1 small onion	1 small onion
½ clove garlic, crushed	½ clove garlic, crushed
generous pinch cumin	generous pinch cumin
seasoning to taste	seasoning to taste
squeeze lemon juice	squeeze lemon juice
1 tablespoon red wine vinegar	1 tablespoon red wine vinegar
pinch raw cane sugar	pinch raw cane sugar
approximately 4 tablespoons soya mayonnaise	approximately 4 tablespoons soy mayonnaise
mint to garnish	mint to garnish

1. Chop the tomatoes and onion. Put them into a heavy-based pan with the garlic, cumin and seasoning.

2. Cook gently, covered, 20-30 minutes or until soft.

3. Rub the purée through a sieve into a clean saucepan. Add the lemon juice, vinegar and sugar. Bring the mixture to a boil then lower the heat and simmer briefly to thicken.

4. Cool, then mix in enough mayonnaise to give the tomato sauce a creamy texture. Transfer to a plastic container and freeze until it begins to set.

5. Beat to lighten and then return it to the freezer and leave to set completely.

6. Crush the tomato ice shortly before you wish to serve it. Spoon into chilled glasses and garnish with mint.

STUFFED MUSHROOMS

Imperial (Metric)	American
8 large field mushrooms (see note)	**8 large field mushrooms (see note)**
3 oz (85g) vegan margarine	**⅓ cup vegan margarine**
½ small onion, chopped	**½ small onion, chopped**
1 oz (30g) fresh wholemeal breadcrumbs	**½ cup fresh whole wheat breadcrumbs**
3 oz (85g) cooked sweetcorn	**⅔ cup cooked corn**
1 oz (30g) sunflower seeds	**¼ cup sunflower seeds**
½ teaspoon marjoram	**½ teaspoon marjoram**
seasoning to taste	**seasoning to taste**
parsley to garnish	**parsley to garnish**

1. Wipe the mushrooms clean and remove and chop the stems.

2. Melt 2 oz (55g) of the margarine in a saucepan. Gently sauté the onion a few minutes, then add the mushroom stems and cook until tender.

3. Remove the pan from the heat and stir in the remaining ingredients, making sure they are thoroughly mixed.

4. Arrange the mushroom caps side by side in a shallow ovenproof dish. Spoon some of the filling into each, piling it up if necessary. Dot each one with the remaining margarine.

5. Bake at 375°F/190°C (Gas Mark 5) about 20 minutes or until the mushrooms are cooked.

6. Serve at once, 2 to each person. Garnish with sprigs of parsley.

NOTE: Field mushrooms have a special flavour, but as they are only available during the late summer and autumn, and then not always easy to obtain, you can always use large flat cultivated mushrooms instead.

Fennel à la Grècque

Imperial (Metric)	American
3 tablespoons vegetable oil (preferably olive)	3 tablespoons vegetable oil (preferably olive)
1 onion, chopped	1 onion, chopped
1 large fennel	1 large fennel
2 tablespoons tomato purée	2 tablespoons tomato paste
1 tablespoon lemon juice	1 tablespoon lemon juice
1 tablespoon red wine vinegar	1 tablespoon red wine vinegar
3 tablespoons water	3 tablespoons water
chopped parsley	chopped parsley
pinch raw cane sugar	pinch raw cane sugar
seasoning to taste	seasoning to taste
1 oz (30g) almonds, coarsely chopped	¼ cup almonds, coarsely chopped

1. Heat the oil in a large pan and sauté the onion a few minutes to soften.

2. Halve the fennel then cut into thin slices.

3. Add to the pan with the tomato purée, lemon juice, vinegar, water, parsley, sugar and seasoning.

4. Bring to a boil, stir, cover and then simmer 20–30 minutes or until the fennel is just cooked.

5. Cool, then refrigerate overnight.

6. Spoon into 4 small dishes or saucers and serve cold garnished with the almonds.

FRUIT SALAD MOULD

Imperial (Metric)	American
1 pint (570ml) apple juice	2½ cups apple juice
2 teaspoons agar agar	2 teaspoons agar agar
½ cucumber	½ cucumber
6 oz (170g) black grapes, halved	1 cup black grapes, halved
2 medium bananas, sliced	2 medium bananas, sliced
1 small grapefruit, segmented	1 small grapefruit, segmented
2 oz (55g) walnuts	½ cup walnuts
watercress to garnish	watercress to garnish

1. Put the juice into a saucepan and bring gently to a boil. Whisk in the agar agar and continue whisking and heating a few minutes more. Set aside to cool briefly.

2. Rinse a medium-sized ring mould with cold water. Slice the cucumber and arrange some of the slices across the base of the mould. Top with grapes then banana slices, some of the grapefruit segments and finally a sprinkling of nuts.

3. Pour in enough fruit juice to cover. Stand the mould in ice water and leave to set.

4. Arrange more layers of cucumber, fruit and nuts and add more of the liquid until all the ingredients are used up. Chill in between each layer so that the ingredients stay in place. If liked, you can arrange the cucumber so that it actually lines the mould rather than making another layer.

5. Finish with liquid then place the mould in the fridge and leave 2 hours at least to set firm.

6. When ready to serve, dip the mould quickly into hot water then invert it so that it slides onto the serving plate. Fill the centre with watercress and take to the table at once.

LEEKS VINAIGRETTE

Imperial (Metric)
8 medium-sized leeks
1-2 tablespoons finely chopped chives, parsley or tarragon
approximately ⅛ (70ml) pint French Dressing (see page 46)
soya "bacon" bits to garnish (optional)

American
8 medium-sized leeks
1-2 tablespoons finely chopped chives, parsley or tarragon
¼ cup French Dressing (see page 46)
soy "bacon" bits to garnish (optional)

1. Trim the leeks, slit lengthways and wash them carefully. Cut into even halves.

2. Place in a wide pan of boiling water and cook until just tender.

3. Drain very well and arrange on a serving dish or 4 individual plates. Mix the herbs into the dressing and spoon a little over each of the leeks.

4. Serve warm or cold garnished, if liked, with crisp soya "bacon" bits.

SALADS

RED CABBAGE SALAD

Imperial (Metric)	American
½ medium red cabbage	½ medium red cabbage
1 large dessert apple	1 large dessert apple
4oz (115g) cooked sweetcorn, drained	⅔ cup cooked corn, drained
½ cucumber	½ cucumber
For French dressing:	For French dressing:
4 tablespoons vegetable oil	4 tablespoons vegetable oil
2 tablespoons cider vinegar	2 tablespoons cider vinegar
pinch dry mustard	pinch dry mustard
seasoning to taste	seasoning to taste
1 oz (30g) coarsely chopped walnuts to garnish	¼ cup coarsely chopped walnuts to garnish
chicory to serve	endive to serve

1. Remove the coarse stalk and any tough outer leaves from the cabbage. Finely shred or grate the cabbage and put it into a bowl.

2. Shred or grate the unpeeled apple and stir into the cabbage with the corn.

3. Make up the dressing by combining all the ingredients in a screwtop jar and shaking well. Pour the dressing over the cabbage and toss lightly. Leave to chill 1 hour.

4. Dice the cucumber and stir it into the cabbage mixture. Spoon into the centre of a deep dish (a soufflé dish is ideal).

5. Arrange chicory (endive) leaves around the edge of the dish. Sprinkle coarsely chopped nuts over the top of the salad, and serve at once.

ENDIVE (CHICORY) WITH BANANA DRESSING

Imperial (Metric)	*American*
1 small endive lettuce	**1 small chicory lettuce**
1 chicory	**1 endive**
1 red pepper	**1 red pepper**
½ bunch watercress	**½ bunch watercress**
For dressing:	*For dressing:*
1 banana	**1 banana**
2–3 tablespoons vegetable oil	**2–3 tablespoons vegetable oil**
1 teaspoon raw cane sugar, powdered in a grinder	**1 teaspoon raw cane sugar, powdered in a grinder**
1 oz (30g) chopped roasted cashew nuts	**¼ cup chopped roasted cashew nuts**

1. Trim the endive (chicory) and remove any damaged leaves. Wash thoroughly, drain well and then tear the leaves into pieces.

2. Slice the chicory (endive) crossways; slice the pepper; trim and wash the watercress.

3. Mix all the vegetables in a bowl.

4. Make the dressing by mashing the banana to a smooth purée then stirring in the oil to give it a softer consistency. Sweeten to taste. Add the nuts.

5. Serve the salad with the dressing spooned over the top. Toss it at the table. A little of the watercress could be reserved to use as a garnish.

KIDNEY BEAN SALAD

Imperial (Metric)	American
½ lb (225g) cooked kidney beans	1 cup cooked kidney beans
½ small cauliflower	½ small cauliflower
1 small leek	1 small leek
2 tomatoes	2 tomatoes
For dressing:	*For dressing:*
4 tablespoons vegetable oil	4 tablespoons vegetable oil
2 tablespoons wine vinegar	2 tablespoons wine vinegar
½ clove garlic, finely chopped	½ clove garlic, finely chopped
¼ teaspoon chilli powder or to taste	¼ teaspoon chili powder or to taste
seasoning to taste	seasoning to taste
lettuce to serve	lettuce to serve
parsley to garnish	parsley to garnish

1. Drain the kidney beans and put into a bowl. Trim the raw cauliflower, cut into florets and stir into the beans.

2. Finely chop the leek and add to the first mixture.

3. Make the dressing by combining all its ingredients in a screwtop jar and shaking well to mix.

4. Pour the dressing over the prepared ingredients, toss lightly, cover and chill at least a few hours, preferably overnight.

5. Just before serving the salad chop the tomatoes coarsely and stir them into the other ingredients.

6. Line a serving bowl with lettuce and pile the bean mixture in the centre. Garnish with parsley and serve at once.

Banana-Rice Ring

Imperial (Metric)	American
½ lb (225g) brown rice	1 cup brown rice
1 pint (570ml) water	2½ cups water
2 bananas	2 bananas
generous squeeze lemon juice	generous squeeze lemon juice
½ green pepper	½ green pepper
2 oz (55g) mushrooms	1 cup mushrooms
2 oz (55g) Brazil nuts	½ cup Brazil nuts
seasoning to taste	seasoning to taste
a few fresh strawberries to garnish	a few fresh strawberries to garnish
lettuce to serve	lettuce to serve

1. Cook the rice in the water about 30 minutes or until well cooked. Drain if necessary. Set aside to cool slightly.

2. Chop the peeled bananas and mix with the lemon juice.

3. Chop the pepper, mushrooms and Brazil nuts.

4. Stir all the ingredients together, making sure they are evenly distributed. Season well.

5. Lightly grease a medium-sized ring mould and spoon in the rice mixture, pressing it down so that it is packed firm. Cover with clingfilm (plastic wrap) and chill 1 hour at least.

6. Remove the wrapping, put a serving plate over the mould, then invert and carefully remove the mould. Garnish the top of the ring with strawberry halves. Arrange lettuce round the edge of the plate. Serve at once.

Carrot and Fruit Salad

Imperial (Metric)	American
3 medium carrots	3 medium carrots
4 oz (115g) dates, finely chopped	⅔ cup dates, finely chopped
4 oz (115g) seedless grapes	¾ cup seedless grapes
1 large dessert apple	1 large dessert apple
1-2 tablespoons lemon juice	1-2 tablespoons lemon juice
1 bunch of watercress	1 bunch of watercress
2 oz (55g) roasted sunflower seeds	⅓ cup roasted sunflower seeds

1. Peel or scrub then coarsely grate the carrots.

2. Mix the carrots with the dates and grapes. Coarsely chop the apple and stir into the other ingredients. Add lemon juice at once and toss lightly.

3. Make a nest of the watercress and spoon the carrot mixture into the centre. Sprinkle with the sunflower seeds. Serve at once.

NOTE: For a more exotic version of this salad, add a creamy dressing to the mixture. The Tofu Dressing (page 66) could be made without the curry powder. Or try the Coconut Dressing (page 57).

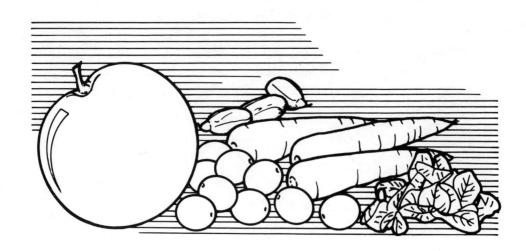

BROCCOLI SALAD WITH MUSTARD CREAM

Imperial (Metric)	American
1½ lbs (680g) broccoli	1½ pounds broccoli
wholemeal croûtons (see page 24)	whole wheat croûtons (see page 24)
For mustard cream:	*For mustard cream:*
½ tablespoon wholemeal flour	½ tablespoon whole wheat flour
2 teaspoons dry mustard	2 teaspoons dry mustard
seasoning to taste	seasoning to taste
generous pinch raw cane sugar	⅔ cup soy milk
¼ pint (140ml) soya milk	¼ cup water
⅛ pint (70ml) water	¼ cup cider vinegar
⅛ pint (70ml) cider vinegar	½ tablespoon vegan margarine
¼ oz (7g) vegan margarine	

1. Trim the broccoli and cut or break into florets. Cook them in a pan of salted boiling water 3–5 minutes only or until just cooked but still crisp. Plunge at once into cold water then drain well and set aside.

2. To make the mustard cream, whisk together all the ingredients and pour into a small pan. Bring to the boil, cook for one minute, then cool.

3. Put the broccoli into a serving dish. Spoon a little of the mustard cream over the top and sprinkle with crisp croûtons. Any extra dressing can be put on the table for those who want it.

Bread Salad (Fattoush)

Imperial (Metric)	American
1 small cucumber	1 small cucumber
1 small crisp lettuce	1 small crisp lettuce
3 tomatoes	3 tomatoes
3 spring onions	3 scallions
½ green pepper	½ green pepper
4 thin slices wholemeal bread	4 thin slices whole wheat bread
For dressing:	*For dressing:*
4 tablespoons vegetable oil	4 tablespoons vegetable oil
2 tablespoons lemon juice	2 tablespoons lemon juice
½ clove garlic, crushed	½ clove garlic, crushed
1 tablespoon chopped fresh coriander leaves	1 tablespoon chopped fresh coriander leaves
½ tablespoon chopped parsley	½ tablespoon chopped parsley
seasoning to taste	seasoning to taste

1. Wash and slice the unpeeled cucumber; wash and shred the lettuce. Coarsely chop the tomatoes, spring onions (scallions) and pepper. Mix all the vegetables together in a salad bowl.

2. Make the dressing by combining all the dressing ingredients in a screwtop jar and shaking well.

3. Pour the dressing over the salad, toss lightly and chill briefly.

4. Toast the bread, allow it to cool then cut into small cubes. Stir them into the salad and serve at once.

MINTED BEETROOT (BEET) SALAD

Imperial (Metric)	American
2 small beetroots (raw)	2 small beets (raw)
2 sticks celery	2 stalks celery
½ small onion	½ small onion
2 oz (55g) raisins	⅓ cup raisins
For dressing:	*For dressing:*
4 tablespoons vegetable oil	4 tablespoons vegetable oil
1 tablespoon lemon juice	1 tablespoon lemon juice
1–2 tablespoons fresh mint, finely chopped	1–2 tablespoons fresh mint, finely chopped
seasoning to taste	seasoning to taste
endive lettuce leaves to serve	chicory lettuce leaves to serve

1. Peel and coarsely grate the beetroots (beets).

2. Finely chop the celery and onion and stir them with the raisins into the grated beetroot (beet).

3. Put all the ingredients for the dressing in a screwtop jar, using enough mint to get the flavour you desire. Shake well to mix.

4. Use most of the salad dressing to moisten the ingredients. Cover the bowl and chill.

5. Just before serving, stir in the rest of the dressing. Line a serving bowl with crisp endive (chicory) leaves, spoon the beetroot (beet) mixture into the centre and serve at once.

NOTE: Young beetroots (beets) are delicious raw. The smaller they are, the sweeter and crisper their flesh is likely to be. When such delicacies are unavailable, cooked ones can also be used in a similar way to that described above, though the finished salad will taste rather different.

LENTIL SALAD WITH ROSEMARY DRESSING

Imperial (Metric)	American
6 oz (170 g) cooked brown lentils	¾ cup cooked brown lentils
2 spring onions	2 scallions
2 young courgettes	2 young zucchini
2 large tomatoes	2 large tomatoes
For dressing:	*For dressing:*
3 tablespoons vegetable oil	3 tablespoons vegetable oil
2 tablespoons lemon juice	2 tablespoons lemon juice
pinch of dry mustard	pinch of dry mustard
1–2 teaspoons fresh rosemary, finely chopped	1–2 teaspoons fresh rosemary, finely chopped
seasoning to taste	seasoning to taste
white cabbage to serve	white cabbage to serve
parsley to garnish	parsley to garnish

1. Drain the lentils well and put them into a bowl (they should be cooked, but not mushy).

2. Chop the spring onions (scallions), courgettes (zucchini) and tomatoes and stir them into the lentils.

3. Make up the salad dressing by putting all its ingredients into a screwtop jar and shaking them until thoroughly mixed.

4. Pour the dressing over the lentil mixture and stir gently. Chill briefly before serving surrounded by shredded white cabbage. Garnish with parsley.

Spinach and "Bacon" Salad

Imperial (Metric)
½ lb (225g) young spinach leaves
2 sticks celery
1 small red pepper
10 green stuffed olives
soya "bacon" bits
For dressing:
½ clove garlic, finely chopped
4 tablespoons olive oil
2 tablespoons wine vinegar
pinch dried basil
seasoning to taste

American
½ pound young spinach leaves
2 stalks celery
1 small red pepper
10 green stuffed olives
soy "bacon" bits
For dressing:
½ clove garlic, finely chopped
4 tablespoons olive oil
2 tablespoons wine vinegar
pinch dried basil
seasoning to taste

1. Wash and shred the spinach. Slice the celery and pepper and coarsely chop the olives.

2. Gently toss together the spinach, celery, pepper and olives.

3. Make up the dressing by combing all the ingredients in a screwtop jar and shaking until well blended. Leave the dressing to stand a while to give the flavours time to mingle.

4. Pour a little of the dressing onto the salad, toss again and sprinkle generously with soya "bacon" bits. Serve at once.

Oriental Pasta Salad

Imperial (Metric)	American
6 oz (170g) wholemeal pasta shells	3 cups whole wheat pasta shells
½ cucumber	½ cucumber
1 large carrot	1 large carrot
1 large stick celery	1 large stalk celery
½ lb (225g) tin pineapple in natural juice	small can pineapple in natural juice
½ bunch watercress	½ bunch watercress
For dressing:	*For dressing:*
2 tablespoons orange juice	2 tablespoons orange juice
½ tablespoon soya sauce	½ tablespoon soy sauce
3–4 tablespoons vegetable oil	3–4 tablespoons vegetable oil
generous pinch ground ginger	generous pinch ground ginger
tamari roasted seeds to garnish (see below)	tamari roasted seeds to garnish (see below)

1. Drop the pasta shells into a saucepan of boiling water and cook 8–10 minutes or until just tender (do not overcook). Drain then drop into cold water. Drain well a second time and set aside.
2. Dice the cucumber; peel and slice the carrot and slice the celery. Drain and coarsely chop the pineapple (reserve the juice).
3. Mix together the pasta, vegetables, pineapple and cleaned, trimmed watercress.
4. Put all the ingredients for the salad dressing into a screwtop jar, adding 2 tablespoons of the pineapple juice. Shake well to mix.
5. Pour a little of the dressing onto the salad, toss gently, chill briefly. Just before serving add the rest of the dressing and sprinkle the top of the salad with the roasted seeds.

For the Tamari Roasted Seeds:	*For the Tamari Roasted Seeds:*
2 oz (55g) pumpkin seeds	½ cup pumpkin seeds
2 oz (55g) sunflower seeds	½ cup sunflower seeds
1 oz (30g) sesame seeds	¼ cup sesame seeds
approximately 2 tablespoons tamari soya sauce	approximately 2 tablespoons tamari soy sauce

1. Mix the seeds then moisten well with the sauce. Stir to make sure they are evenly coated.
2. Put the seeds under a medium-hot grill and cook, stirring frequently, until they are crisp and brown. The sauce will dry to form a delicious coating.
3. Cool the seeds and use as needed. They can be stored in an airtight container if not all of them are needed at once.

PEACH WALDORF

Imperial (Metric)	American
2 large, ripe but firm peaches	2 large, ripe but firm peaches
squeeze lemon juice	squeeze lemon juice
2 large sticks celery	2 large stalks celery
1 small green pepper	1 small green pepper
2 oz (55g) walnuts	½ cup walnuts
small iceberg lettuce	small iceberg lettuce
vegan soft "cheese" (see below)	vegan soft "cheese" (see below)
For "cheese":	*For "cheese":*
1 pint (570ml) soya milk	2½ cups soy milk
2 tablespoons lemon juice	2 tablespoons lemon juice
seasoning to taste	seasoning to taste
For dressing:	*For dressing:*
⅛ pint (70ml) undiluted soya milk	¼ cup undiluted soy milk
1 teaspoon raw cane sugar, powdered in grinder	1 teaspoon raw cane sugar, powdered in grinder
3 tablespoons desiccated coconut or to taste	3 tablespoons desiccated coconut or to taste

1. Carefully cut each peach into 8 segments and brush them lightly with lemon juice.

2. Chop the celery, pepper and walnuts. Stir together.

3. Make a nest of shredded lettuce on 4 plates; top each one with some of the vegetable-and-nut mixture.

4. Put a spoonful of "cheese" on the top of each plate, and arrange the prepared peach segments decoratively around it.

5. In a screwtop jar combine the ingredients for the dressing, shaking well so that they are thoroughly mixed. Adjust the taste.

6. Pour a little of the dressing over each salad and serve at once.

To make the "cheese":

1. Combine the soya milk and lemon juice in a small saucepan. Heat very gently, stirring occasionally, until the mixture begins to curdle.

2. Pour into a piece of muslin or cheesecloth. Secure to make a bag, suspend it over a bowl and leave to drain a few hours, preferably overnight.

3. Season to taste and use within a day or two, refrigerating the "cheese" if not required immediately.

POTATO SALAD WITH HAZELNUTS

Imperial (Metric)
1 lb (455g) new potatoes
1 small fennel bulb
3 oz (85g) chopped roasted
hazelnuts
For dressing:
3 tablespoons olive oil
1 tablespoon cider vinegar
seasoning to taste
fennel leaves to garnish

American
1 pound new potatoes
1 small fennel bulb
⅔ cup chopped roasted hazelnuts
For dressing:
3 tablespoons olive oil
1 tablespoon cider vinegar
seasoning to taste
fennel leaves to garnish

1. Steam or boil the unpeeled potatoes until just cooked but still firm. Set them aside to cool. (Peel them carefully while still warm if you do not want the skins left on, though they do add taste, texture and nutrients to the salad.)

2. Trim and coarsely chop the fennel. (This is best left raw, but if you prefer it softer, cook briefly with the potatoes.)

3. Cube the potatoes and mix with the fennel and hazelnuts.

4. Lightly whisk together the oil, vinegar and seasoning and pour it over the potatoes. Stir gently.

5. Set aside briefly until completely cold. Serve garnished with fennel leaves.

CUCUMBER RATATOUILLE

Imperial (Metric)

4 tablespoons vegetable oil
2 onions, peeled and chopped
1 clove garlic, crushed
3 tomatoes, coarsely chopped
1 cucumber, diced
1 green pepper, diced
1 aubergine, diced
seasoning to taste
1½ oz (45g) pine nuts to garnish
parsley to garnish

American

4 tablespoons vegetable oil
2 onions, peeled and chopped
1 clove garlic, crushed
3 tomatoes, coarsely chopped
1 cucumber, diced
1 green pepper, diced
1 eggplant, diced
seasoning to taste
3 tablespoons pine nuts to garnish
parsley to garnish

1. Heat the oil in a large pan. Add the onions, garlic and tomatoes.

2. Cook gently 10 minutes.

3. Add the cucumber, pepper and aubergine (eggplant). Stir well. Season.

4. Cover the pan and simmer gently 40 minutes or until the vegetables are just cooked.

5. Chill well. Serve garnished with pine nuts and a good sprinkling of fresh chopped parsley.

ROOT VEGETABLE SALAD

Imperial (Metric)	American
4 oz (115g) carrots	1 large carrot (about 4 ounces)
4 oz (115g) parsnips	1 medium-sized parsnip (about 4 ounces)
4 oz (115g) turnips	1 small turnip (about 4 ounces)
4 small Brussels sprouts	4 small Brussels sprouts
For dressing:	*For dressing:*
2 tablespoons smooth peanut butter	2 tablespoons smooth peanut butter
2 tablespoons lemon juice	2 tablespoons lemon juice
4–5 tablespoons vegetable oil	4–5 tablespoons vegetable oil
seasoning to taste	seasoning to taste
lettuce to serve	lettuce to serve
1 oz (30g) salted peanuts	3 tablespoons salted peanuts

1. Peel the carrots, parsnips and turnips. Trim the Brussels sprouts.

2. Coarsely grate all the vegetables into a bowl.

3. Stir together the peanut butter, lemon juice and oil so that they are thoroughly blended. Adjust the consistency, if necessary, with a little extra lemon juice or oil. Season to taste.

4. Pour the dressing over the vegetables and toss lightly to spread the dressing evenly.

5. Serve at once on a bed of pale, crisp lettuce. Garnish with extra peanuts.

BEANSPROUT SALAD

Imperial (Metric)	American
6 oz (170g) beansprouts	3 cups beansprouts
2 sticks celery, finely sliced	2 stalks celery, finely sliced
1 red pepper, finely sliced	1 red pepper, finely sliced
2 oz (55g) cooked peas	⅓ cup cooked peas
2 oz (55g) roasted flaked almonds	½ cup roasted slivered almonds
For dressing:	*For dressing:*
2 tablespoons lemon juice	2 tablespoons lemon juice
2 tablespoons wine vinegar	2 tablespoons wine vinegar
generous pinch raw cane sugar	generous pinch raw cane sugar
1 teaspoon soya sauce or to taste	1 teaspoon soy sauce or to taste
watercress to garnish	watercress to garnish

1. Wash and drain the beansprouts well and put into a bowl.

2. Stir in the celery and pepper; drain and add the peas and then most of the nuts.

3. Put all the ingredients for the dressing into a screwtop jar and shake until well mixed. (If the sugar is first powdered in a grinder, this will be easier to do.)

4. Pour the dressing over the salad, stir gently and chill briefly. Serve topped with a generous garnish of watercress and the remaining nuts.

Melon Avocado Salad

Imperial (Metric)	American
½ lb (225g) tomatoes	½ pound tomatoes
2 ripe but firm avocados	2 ripe but firm avocados
1 ripe but firm medium-sized melon	1 ripe but firm medium-sized melon
generous squeeze lemon juice	generous squeeze lemon juice
2 oz (55g) pecan nuts	½ cup pecan nuts

1. Wipe the tomatoes to clean, then cut them crossways into even slices. Arrange these around the edge of an attractive serving plate.

2. Peel and cube the avocado; do the same with the melon. Toss both gently in the lemon juice. Mix in most of the nuts.

3. Spoon the melon-avocado mixture into the centre of the plate and top with the remaining nuts. Serve at once.

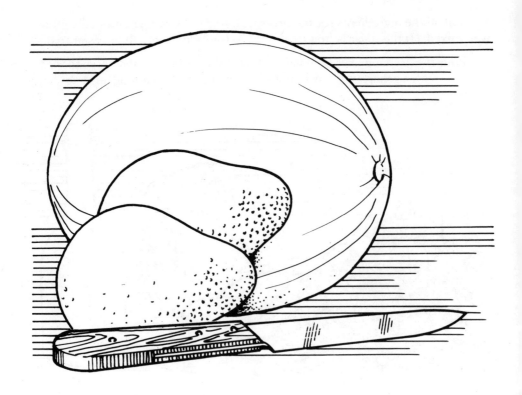

Artichokes Niçoise

Imperial (Metric)	American
6 globe artichokes	6 globe artichokes
½ green pepper	½ green pepper
3 large tomatoes	3 large tomatoes
12 black olives	12 black olives
1 tablespoon capers	1 tablespoon capers
For dressing:	*For dressing:*
½ clove garlic, finely chopped	½ clove garlic, finely chopped
6 tablespoons vegetable oil	6 tablespoons vegetable oil
2 tablespoons wine or cider vinegar	2 tablespoons wine or cider vinegar
½ teaspoon made-up mustard	½ teaspoon prepared mustard
seasoning to taste	seasoning to taste
parsley or watercress to garnish	parsley or watercress to garnish

1. Wash the artichokes carefully under running water, remove the outer leaves and cut off the stems. Trim any remaining leaves above the base of the hearts. Cook in a pan of boiling salted water 30–40 minutes or until a leaf comes out easily when pulled. When cooked, stand the artichokes upside down to drain.

2. When cold, remove the artichoke leaves and the chokes. Cut the remaining hearts into quarters. Put them into a bowl.

3. Thinly slice the pepper and chop the tomatoes. Add them to the bowl. Stir in the olives and capers.

4. Put the ingredients for the dressing into a screwtop jar and shake well to combine. Pour enough of the dressing over the salad ingredients to moisten, toss lightly and chill briefly before serving.

NOTE: When fresh artichokes are not available, this recipe can be followed using tinned ones instead.

CHINESE COLESLAW WITH NUTMEAT

Imperial (Metric)	*American*
1 small Chinese cabbage	1 small Chinese cabbage
2 large carrots, grated	2 large carrots, grated
2 oz (55g) beansprouts	1 cup beansprouts
1 small dessert apple	1 small dessert apple
squeeze of lemon juice	squeeze of lemon juice
small tin of nutmeat, cubed	small can textured nutmeat, cubed
For dressing:	*For dressing:*
5 tablespoons vegetable oil	5 tablespoons vegetable oil
2 tablespoons wine vinegar	2 tablespoons wine vinegar
1–2 spring onions, finely chopped	1–2 scallions, finely chopped
seasoning to taste	seasoning to taste

1. Wash, drain and slice the cabbage. Put it into a large bowl.

2. Add the carrots and the beansprouts. Coarsely chop the apple and toss it in the lemon juice, then add it to the bowl.

3. In a screwtop jar combine the oil, vinegar, spring onions (scallions) and seasoning. Pour dressing over salad ingredients and mix thoroughly.

4. Pile the salad into a serving bowl. Top with the nutmeat. Serve at once.

WATERCRESS AND ORANGE SALAD

Imperial (Metric)	American
2 bunches watercress	2 bunches watercress
2 oranges	2 oranges
3 sticks celery	3 stalks celery
2 oz (55g) raisins	⅓ cup raisins
3 oz (85g) Brazil nut pieces	¾ cup Brazil nut pieces
lettuce for base	lettuce for base
For dressing:	*For dressing:*
4 tablespoons vegetable oil	⅓ cup vegetable oil
2 tablespoons wine vinegar	2 tablespoons wine vinegar
pinch dry mustard	pinch dry mustard
pinch raw cane sugar	pinch raw cane sugar
seasoning to taste	seasoning to taste

1. Wash and trim the watercress; peel and slice the oranges; chop the celery into small pieces.

2. Mix all the salad ingredients together; add raisins and nuts.

3. Combine the ingredients for the dressing in a screwtop jar and shake well. Pour a little over the prepared ingredients; place the salad on the lettuce base and put the rest of the dressing on the table for those who like more.

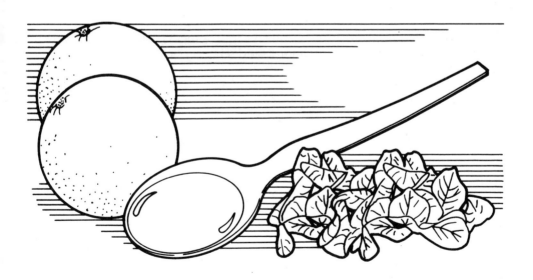

FRENCH BEAN SALAD WITH TOFU DRESSING

Imperial (Metric)	American
¾ lb (340g) French beans	¾ pound green beans
4 oz (115g) button mushrooms, sliced	2 cups button mushrooms, sliced
2 oz (55g) roasted flaked almonds	½ cup roasted slivered almonds
For dressing:	*For dressing:*
4 oz (115g) tofu	½ cup tofu
2 tablespoons lemon juice	2 tablespoons lemon juice
2 tablespoons vegetable oil	2 tablespoons vegetable oil
½ teaspoon curry powder or to taste	½ teaspoon curry powder or to taste
seasoning to taste	seasoning to taste

1. Top and tail the beans and, if necessary, trim the sides. Cut them diagonally into short, even-sized slices. Cook in a pan of boiling salted water 5–10 minutes then drain well.

2. Plunge the beans at once into very cold water. Drain again, making sure they are as dry as possible.

3. Put them into a serving bowl and stir in the mushrooms.

4. Use a blender to make a smooth thick purée with the ingredients for the dressing, adjusting the consistency and taste to suit yourself. (You can also make it by mashing the tofu with a fork, then whisking in the remaining ingredients, but it will not be as smooth.)

5. Spoon the dressing onto the vegetables and toss them gently. Sprinkle with the roasted almonds and serve at once.

Bulgur Salad

Imperial (Metric)	American
6 oz (170g) bulgur	¾ cup bulgur
2 sticks celery	2 stalks celery
2 spring onions	2 scallions
12 radishes	12 radishes
2 oz (55g) mushrooms	1 cup mushrooms
2 oz (55g) peanuts	3½ tablespoons peanuts
2 tablespoons chopped parsley	2 tablespoons chopped parsley
watercress to garnish	watercress to garnish
For dressing:	*For dressing:*
3 tablespoons vegetable oil	3 tablespoons vegetable oil
3 tablespoons lemon juice	3 tablespoons lemon juice
seasoning to taste	seasoning to taste

1. Put the bulgur in a bowl and cover with cold water. Leave to soak at least 30 minutes then drain well before putting it into a piece of muslin, cheesecloth or clean tea towel, squeezing to remove any remaining water.

2. Finely chop the celery and spring onions (scallions). Slice the radishes and mushrooms. Stir the prepared vegetables into the bulgur with the nuts and parsley.

3. Add the oil and lemon juice and toss lightly so that the dressing is well distributed. Season to taste. Serve at once garnished with watercress.

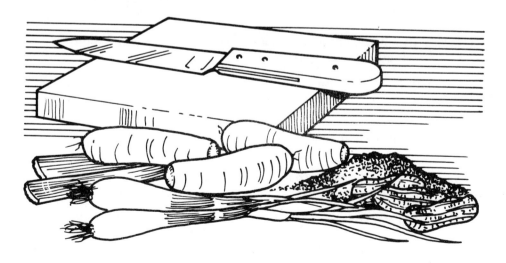

IDEAS FROM AROUND THE WORLD

SPAGHETTI VERONESE

Imperial (Metric)	American
2–3 tablespoons vegetable oil (preferably olive)	2–3 tablespoons vegetable oil (preferably olive)
1 onion, chopped	1 onion, chopped
½–1 clove garlic, crushed	½–1 clove garlic, crushed
1 tablespoon chopped parsley	1 tablespoon chopped parsley
6 oz (170g) peas, fresh or frozen	1 cup peas, fresh or frozen
½ lb (225g) mushrooms, cleaned and sliced	4 cups mushrooms, cleaned and sliced
soya "bacon" bits	soy "bacon" bits
seasoning to taste	seasoning to taste
¾ lb (340g) wholemeal spaghetti	12 ounces whole wheat spaghetti
parsley to garnish	parsley to garnish

1. Heat the oil in a frying pan and gently cook the onion and garlic a few minutes. Add the parsley and cook a few minutes more.

2. Stir in the peas adding just a few spoonsful of water. (If they are frozen you may not need extra water.) Cover the pan and cook gently 5 minutes, taking care they do not dry out.

3. Add the mushrooms and stir well. Cook 5–10 minutes more, until the vegetables are tender.

4. Meanwhile drop the spaghetti into a large pan of boiling, salted water, lower the heat and cook 10 minutes or until just tender.

5. Drain the pasta and arrange on a serving dish. (Wholemeal pasta does not need to be rinsed through.)

6. Add the "bacon" bits to the sauce, season to taste and pour it over the spaghetti. Garnish with more parsley and serve at once.

NOTE: Spaghetti Veronese is traditionally made with bacon, but if you prefer to avoid the taste fry some almonds in oil until golden, then chop coarsely and use them instead of the "bacon" bits. The nuts add a nice crunchy texture.

Sweet and Sour "Chicken"

Imperial (Metric)	American
3 tablespoons vegetable oil	3 tablespoons vegetable oil
1 large onion, sliced	1 large onion, sliced
1 large green pepper, sliced	1 large green pepper, sliced
1 oz (30g) wholemeal flour	¼ cup whole wheat flour
½ lb (225g) tin pineapple in natural juice	small can pineapple in natural juice
⅛ pint (70ml) wine vinegar	¼ cup wine vinegar
pinch dry mustard	pinch dry mustard
1 oz (30g) raw cane sugar	2 tablespoons raw cane sugar
Holbrook's Worcester sauce	vegetarian Worcester sauce
1–2 tablespoons soya sauce	1–2 tablespoons soy sauce
seasoning to taste	seasoning to taste
5 oz (140g) soya "chicken" pieces, hydrated in water	1¼ cups soy "chicken" pieces, hydrated in water
small bunch seedless grapes	small bunch seedless grapes

1. Heat the oil in a pan and sauté the onion and pepper 10 minutes, stirring often.

2. Put the flour in a bowl. Drain the juice from the pineapple and add water to make up to ½ pint (285ml) of liquid. Mix with the flour, vinegar, mustard, sugar, Worcester sauce, soya sauce and seasoning.

3. Pour into the pan, bring to a boil then simmer gently a few minutes to thicken the sauce.

4. Drain and add the "chicken" pieces; coarsely chop the pineapple and add with the grapes. Stir well then simmer 10 minutes. Serve with rice or other grain dish.

PISSALADIÈRES

Imperial (Metric)	American
For pastry:	*For pastry:*
½ lb (225g) wholemeal flour	2 cups whole wheat flour
pinch of salt	pinch of salt
4 oz (115g) vegan margarine	½ cup vegan margarine
3–4 tablespoons cold water	3–4 tablespoons cold water
For filling:	*For filling:*
3 tablespoons vegetable oil	3 tablespoons vegetable oil
3 onions, finely chopped	3 onions, finely chopped
1–2 cloves garlic, crushed	1–2 cloves garlic, crushed
1 lb (455g) tomatoes, peeled and chopped	1 pound tomatoes, peeled and chopped
2 tablespoons tomato purée	2 tablespoons tomato paste
seasoning to taste	seasoning to taste
24 black olives	24 black olives

1. Sift together the flour and salt. Rub in the margarine to make a crumb-like mixture, then stir in the water to form a dough. Wrap it in clingfilm (plastic wrap) and chill 30 minutes.

2. Roll out the dough and cut into 8 fairly large circles, using these to line lightly greased tartlet tins. Prick the bases. Bake at 375°F/190°C (Gas Mark 5) 10–15 minutes, or until cooked.

3. Meanwhile prepare the filling. Heat the oil and fry the onions with the garlic 5 minutes or until soft but not browned.

4. Add the tomatoes with the purée and seasoning. Stir well and cook no more than 5 minutes, to just soften and heat the tomatoes.

5. Spoon the hot filling into the hot or warm cases and decorate with 3 olives for each tart. Serve at once, possibly with a salad which includes nuts or beans and a protein-rich dressing.

NOTE: One garlic clove gives a good flavour, but two give the more traditional taste of French cookery. Pissaladières can also be served cold.

Mexican Bulgur

Imperial (Metric)	American
2 tablespoons vegetable oil	**2 tablespoons vegetable oil**
1 onion, chopped	**1 onion, chopped**
1 green pepper, chopped	**1 green pepper, chopped**
½ lb (225g) bulgur	**1 cup bulgur**
4 oz (115g) cooked sweetcorn, drained	**⅔ cup cooked corn, drained**
3 tomatoes, chopped	**3 tomatoes, chopped**
¾ pint (425ml) vegetable stock	**2 cups vegetable stock**
½ teaspoon chilli powder or to taste	**½ teaspoon chili powder or to taste**
seasoning to taste	**seasoning to taste**
1 large firm avocado	**1 large firm avocado**

1. Heat the vegetable oil in a saucepan. Sauté the onion and pepper 5 minutes.

2. Add the bulgur, stir and cook gently a few minutes more.

3. Stir in the corn, tomatoes, vegetable stock and chilli powder. Bring to a boil then lower the heat, cover the pan and simmer about 15 minutes or until all the stock has been absorbed. Season to taste.

4. Peel the avocado and chop into chunks, stir into the other ingredients and serve at once.

MUSHROOM GOULASH

Imperial (Metric)	American
2 tablespoons vegetable oil	2 tablespoons vegetable oil
2 onions, chopped	2 onions, chopped
¾ lb (340g) mushrooms	¾ pound mushrooms
½ oz (15g) wholemeal flour	2 tablespoons whole wheat flour
1 tablespoon paprika	1 tablespoon paprika
½ pint (285ml) vegetable stock	1⅓ cups vegetable stock
3 tomatoes	3 tomatoes
1 small green pepper	1 small green pepper
seasoning to taste	seasoning to taste
approximately ⅛ pint (70ml) undiluted soya milk	approximately ¼ cup undiluted soy milk
parsley to garnish	parsley to garnish

1. Heat the oil and sauté the onions 5 minutes to soften.

2. Clean and thickly slice the mushrooms and stir in, sautéing gently a few minutes more. Then add the flour and paprika and cook until beginning to change colour.

3. Pour in the vegetable stock. Peel and chop the tomatoes, slice the pepper and add these to the saucepan. Bring the mixture to a boil, cover and simmer 20–30 minutes or until all the ingredients are tender.

4. Remove the saucepan from the heat and stir in enough undiluted soya (soy) milk to give a creamy texture. Serve at once garnished with parsley.

TOFU CURRY (THAILAND)

Imperial (Metric)	American
10 oz (285g) tofu	1 ¼ cups tofu
3–4 tablespoons vegetable oil	3–4 tablespoons vegetable oil
2 large onions, sliced	2 large onions, sliced
2 shallots	2 shallots
2 cloves garlic	2 cloves garlic
1 inch (25mm) knob Siamese ginger	1 inch knob ginger
¾ inch (20mm) stalk lemon grass	¾ inch stalk lemon grass
2 teaspoons chopped coriander root	2 teaspoons chopped coriander root
10 dried red chillies	10 dried red chilies
½ teaspoon grated lime peel	½ teaspoon grated lime peel
3 teaspoons roasted coriander seeds	3 teaspoons roasted coriander seeds
1 teaspoon roasted cumin seeds	1 teaspoon roasted cumin seeds
2 roasted cardamom seeds	2 roasted cardamom seeds
½ teaspoon ground nutmeg	½ teaspoon ground nutmeg
½ teaspoon ground cinnamon	½ teaspoon ground cinnamon
½ teaspoon ground cloves	½ teaspoon ground cloves
¼ teaspoon ground mace	¼ teaspoon ground mace
scant ½ pint (285ml) thick coconut milk	scant 1 ⅓ cups thick coconut milk
2 tablespoons tamarind water	2 tablespoons tamarind water
level tablespoon raw cane sugar	level tablespoon raw cane sugar
seasoning to taste	seasoning to taste

1. Drain the tofu well. Cut it into cubes and sauté in some of the oil, turning occasionally. When lightly browned, remove it from the pan and set aside.

2. Add more oil if necessary, sauté the onion in the same way and set aside.

3. Finely chop the shallots, garlic, ginger and lemon grass.

4. In a mortar and pestle grind these with the coriander root, chillies, lime peel, coriander seeds, cumin seeds and cardamom seeds. Add the ground spices. Stir in a few spoonsful of cold water to make a paste.

5. Heat more oil in the same pan then add the paste and stir well; sauté a few minutes, stirring frequently.

6. Pour in the coconut milk and bring to a boil. Add the tamarind water, sugar and seasoning. Boil again before stirring in the tofu and onions.

7. Simmer 10 minutes. Serve with rice.

NOTE: This recipe was recommended to me by Mr S. Klinpikuln of Bath— whose cookery deserves a recommendation of its own! He explains that most if not all of the ingredients should be available in oriental supermarkets. Some substitutions can be made—for example, lime juice could be used in place of the tamarind water, ready mixed chilli paste instead of the dried chillies. If just one of the ingredients used to flavour the sauce is completely unobtainable, it can be left out without ruining the dish. The result, of course, will not be exactly the same as the genuine dish, but the difference would probably only be noticed by those who are familiar with Thai food.

FALAFELS WITH HUMMUS

Imperial (Metric)	American
½ lb (225g) chickpeas, soaked overnight	1⅓ cups chickpeas, soaked overnight
seasoning to taste	seasoning to taste
1-2 cloves garlic, crushed	1-2 cloves garlic, crushed
1 tablespoon fresh coriander leaves, chopped	1 tablespoon fresh coriander leaves, chopped
½ teaspoon cumin	½ teaspoon cumin
½ teaspoon turmeric	½ teaspoon turmeric
pinch chilli powder (optional)	pinch chili powder (optional)
½ green pepper	½ green pepper
vegetable oil for cooking	vegetable oil for cooking
For hummus:	*For hummus:*
6 oz (170g) chickpeas, soaked overnight	1 cup chickpeas, soaked overnight
¼ pint (140ml) tahini	⅔ cup tahini
2 tablespoons lemon juice	2 tablespoons lemon juice
1 clove garlic, crushed	1 clove garlic, crushed
seasoning to taste	seasoning to taste
olive oil	olive oil
black olives and parsley to garnish	black olives and parsley to garnish

1. For the falafels the chickpeas should be just soft enough to grind. This is best achieved by soaking them in water in which they have first been boiled 10 minutes. (Or cook them briefly.) Rub off the skins. Grind the chickpeas as fine as possible and put them in a bowl.

2. Add seasoning, garlic, coriander leaves and spices. Chop the pepper very fine and add to the mixture. Blend thoroughly then chill briefly. (You can combine all the ingredients in a blender if you prefer.)

3. Shape the mixture into small balls. Deep or shallow fry them until crisp and brown. Drain and serve the falafels with hummus, pita bread and a salad.

4. To make the hummus, cover the chickpeas with fresh water, boil 10 minutes then lower the heat and simmer, covered, about 1½ hours or until well cooked.

5. Drain the chickpeas and grind them to a smooth paste. Add a drop of the liquid in which they were cooked, the tahini, lemon juice, garlic and seasoning. Stir well to make a thick creamy purée (add extra liquid if necessary). Adjust the flavouring to taste.

6. Spoon into a dish, trickle oil over the top and garnish with olives and parsley.

NOTE: Falafel also go well with a sauce made just from tahini, lemon juice, water and seasoning plus a few chopped olives if liked.

GADO GADO (PEANUT SAUCE)

Imperial (Metric)
3 tablespoons vegetable oil
1 onion, finely chopped
1-2 cloves garlic, crushed
1 teaspoon grated ginger root
6 oz (170g) smooth peanut butter
1 pint (570ml) vegetable stock or
water
juice of 1 lemon
½ teaspoon chilli powder
½ teaspoon raw cane sugar
seasoning to taste
2-3 tablespoons soya milk
(optional)

American
3 tablespoons vegetable oil
1 onion, finely chopped
1-2 cloves garlic, crushed
1 teaspoon grated ginger root
1½ cups smooth peanut butter
2½ cups vegetable stock or water
juice of 1 lemon
½ teaspoon chili powder
½ teaspoon raw cane sugar
seasoning to taste
2-3 tablespoons soy milk
(optional)

1. Heat the oil and sauté the onion with the garlic and ginger. When they are soft but not browned use a wooden spoon to stir in the peanut butter.

2. Add the vegetable stock and continue stirring over a gentle heat until the peanut butter dissolves completely.

3. Add the lemon juice, chilli powder, sugar and seasoning. Simmer about 15 minutes, stirring occasionally. The sauce should have a pouring consistency—if it is too thick, adjust with more water.

4. If a creamier texture is liked add the soya milk at the very last moment. Pour into a jug and take to the table at once.

NOTE: Gado gado is served over a bed of vegetables, either cooked or raw, usually accompanied by a grain such as rice, buckwheat or millet. Garnishes can include roasted peanuts, flaked coconut, banana chunks etc.

CREOLE JAMBALAYA

Imperial (Metric)	American
5 oz (140g) soya "ham" chunks, hydrated in water	1¼ cups soy "ham" chunks, hydrated in water
2–3 tablespoons vegetable oil	2–3 tablespoons vegetable oil
1 green pepper, sliced	1 green pepper, sliced
2 small onions, sliced	2 small onions, sliced
1 clove garlic, crushed	1 clove garlic, crushed
1 cup celery leaves	1 cup celery leaves
14 oz (395g) tin tomatoes	medium can tomatoes
3 tablespoons tomato purée	3 tablespoons tomato purée
few drops Holbrook's Worcester sauce	few drops vegetarian Worcester sauce
½ lb (225g) brown rice	1 cup brown rice
approximately ⅓ pint (200ml) vegetable stock	approximately ¾ cup vegetable stock
½ teaspoon thyme	½ teaspoon thyme
seasoning to taste	seasoning to taste
fresh chopped parsley to garnish	fresh chopped parsley to garnish

1. Drain the "ham" chunks and cook gently in half the oil, turning occasionally, until they begin to colour. Remove them from the pan and set aside.

2. Add more oil if necessary then sauté the pepper, onions and garlic until they begin to soften.

3. Add the celery leaves and cook a minute or two. Drain and coarsely chop the tomatoes and add with the purée; stir well and flavour with a few drops of sauce.

4. Wash and stir in the rice plus the stock, thyme and seasoning. Bring to a boil and add the "ham" chunks. Cover the pan and cook gently about 20 minutes or until the rice is tender. Check that it does not stick during the cooking process and add a drop more stock if necessary.

5. Serve garnished with plenty of fresh parsley.

NOTE: Authentic Creole Jambalaya has prawns or shrimps in it. If you feel the contrast they make is important, try sprinkling in a handful of cashew nuts.

ALMOND VEGETABLE CHOP SUEY

Imperial (Metric)	American
3 spring onions	3 scallions
1 red pepper	1 red pepper
3 oz (85g) mushrooms	1½ cups mushrooms
⅛ small white cabbage	⅛ small white cabbage
1 stick celery	1 stalk celery
½ bunch watercress	½ bunch watercress
½ tablespoon arrowroot or wholemeal flour	½ tablespoon arrowroot or whole wheat flour
⅛ pint (70ml) cold water	¼ cup cold water
soya sauce to taste	soy sauce to taste
2–3 tablespoons vegetable oil	2–3 tablespoons vegetable oil
3 oz (85g) almonds	¾ cup almonds
1 teaspoon dry sherry	1 teaspoon dry sherry
4 oz (115g) beansprouts	2 cups beansprouts

1. Slice the spring onions (scallions), pepper, mushrooms, cabbage and celery. Wash the watercress and remove the stems.

2. In a small bowl whisk together the arrowroot, water and enough soya sauce to give a rich colour.

3. Heat the oil in a large heavy-based frying pan or wok. Add the spring onions and pepper and cook 3 minutes. Add the mushrooms and cook 1–2 minutes more.

4. Add the remaining vegetables and the almonds. Cook 5 minutes stirring occasionally. The vegetables should be cooked but still crisp.

5. Pour in the arrowroot mixture, stir then cook over low heat until the sauce thickens, adding the sherry and a drop more water if necessary.

6. Add the beansprouts and leave on the heat for literally 1 minute to warm through. Serve at once. Rice is a traditional base, but millet goes well and makes an interesting change.

WALNUT MOUSSAKA

Imperial (Metric)	American
1 large aubergine	1 large eggplant
approximately 5 tablespoons vegetable oil	approximately 5 tablespoons vegetable oil
1 large onion, chopped	1 large onion, chopped
4 oz (115g) mushrooms, chopped	2 cups mushrooms, chopped
4 tomatoes	4 tomatoes
1 tablespoon tomato purée	1 tablespoon tomato purée
2 tablespoons red wine (optional)	2 tablespoons red wine (optional)
1 teaspoon mixed herbs	1 teaspoon mixed herbs
3 oz (85g) walnuts, ground	¾ cup walnuts, ground
1 oz (30g) wholemeal breadcrumbs	½ cup whole wheat breadcrumbs
garlic salt	garlic salt
pepper	pepper
1 oz (30g) wholemeal flour	¼ cup whole wheat flour
½ pint (285ml) soya milk	1⅓ cups soy milk
extra walnuts and parsley to garnish	extra walnuts and parsley to garnish

1. Slice the aubergine (eggplant) as thin as possible. Sprinkle with salt and set aside 30 minutes then rinse well in cold water and pat dry.

2. Heat 2 tablespoons of oil and sauté the aubergine slices on both sides. Drain on paper towels.

3. Add a drop more oil to the pan and sauté the onion 5 minutes to soften. Add the mushrooms, stir and cook 5 minutes more.

4. Peel and chop the tomatoes and add them to the pan with the purée. Add the wine, if using it, and the herbs. Cook gently until a sauce begins to form.

5. Stir in the nuts and breadcrumbs.

6. Flavour with garlic salt and pepper. If the mixture seems very dry add a drop of oil, vegetable stock or tomato purée mixed with water.

7. Make a white sauce by heating 1 tablespoon of oil in a pan and sprinkling in the flour. Cook briefly, then stir in the soya milk and cook gently until the sauce thickens. Season to taste.

8. Arrange half the aubergine across the base of a lightly greased shallow ovenproof dish. Top with half the nut mixture then half the sauce. Repeat to use up the remaining ingredients.

9. Bake at 350°F/180°C (Gas Mark 4) 15 minutes. Sprinkle the top with a few extra walnuts and continue cooking 15 minutes more. Serve hot, sprinkled with plenty of parsley.

LENTIL DHAL

Imperial (Metric)	American
½ lb (225g) split red lentils	1 cup split red lentils
1–2 cloves garlic, crushed	1–2 cloves garlic, crushed
½ teaspoon garam masala	½ teaspoon garam masala (pre-
3 tablespoons vegetable oil	mixed Indian spice)
1 large onion, chopped	3 tablespoons vegetable oil
1–2 teaspoons ground cumin	1 large onion, chopped
generous pinch asafoetida powder	1–2 teaspoons ground cumin
chopped coriander leaves to	generous pinch asafoetida powder
garnish (optional)	chopped coriander leaves to
	garnish (optional)

1. Put the lentils, garlic and garam masala in a saucepan. Cover well with boiling water. Simmer until the lentils are well cooked then drain off excess liquid. Stir the lentils with a wooden spoon to make a thick, smooth purée.

2. In another saucepan heat most of the oil and sauté the onion until golden brown. Stir it into the lentil mixture and continue cooking briefly.

3. Still using the second pan heat the remaining oil. Add the cumin and asafoetida, stir well and cook literally ½ minute. Mix this into the lentils.

4. Serve at once garnished, if possible, with fresh coriander leaves.

CANNELLONI FLORENTINE

Imperial (Metric)	American
1 lb (455g) spinach	1 pound spinach
2 tablespoons vegetable oil	2 tablespoons vegetable oil
1 small onion, chopped	1 small onion, chopped
½ clove garlic, crushed	½ clove garlic, crushed
10 oz (285g) tofu	1 ¼ cups tofu
generous pinch nutmeg	generous pinch nutmeg
seasoning to taste	seasoning to taste
12 small cannelloni tubes	12 small cannelloni tubes
For tomato sauce:	*For tomato sauce:*
14 oz (395g) tin tomatoes	medium can tomatoes
1 large carrot	1 large carrot
1 onion	1 onion
2 sticks celery	2 stalks celery
1 tablespoon tomato purée	1 tablespoon tomato paste
1 teaspoon raw cane sugar	1 teaspoon raw cane sugar
1 teaspoon chopped basil	1 teaspoon chopped basil
seasoning to taste	seasoning to taste

1. Wash and coarsely shred the spinach. Put into a saucepan without adding extra water, cover and cook gently a few minutes until wilted. Drain and chop fine.

2. Heat the oil and sauté the onion and garlic until lightly browned.

3. Drain and mash the tofu. Add it to the saucepan with the nutmeg and seasoning. Mix well and cook a few minutes more. Add the spinach.

4. Use the mixture to stuff the cannelloni tubes. Lay them side by side in a lightly greased ovenproof dish.

5. To make the sauce, first crush or liquidize the tomatoes, finely grate the carrot and onion and chop the celery. Combine these with all the remaining ingredients in a saucepan, bring to a boil then cover the pan and simmer 20–30 minutes.

6. Spread the sauce evenly over the cannelloni. Bake at 400°F/200°C (Gas Mark 6) 20 minutes.

NOTE: Ready-made cannelloni tubes vary in that some of them need to be cooked before they are filled; others can be filled straight away. Check the instructions on the package.

BOSTON BAKED BEANS

Imperial (Metric)	American
½ lb (225g) haricot beans, soaked overnight	1 cup navy beans, soaked overnight
2 tablespoons vegetable oil	2 tablespoons vegetable oil
2 onions, chopped	2 onions, chopped
1 lb (455g) tomatoes, peeled and chopped	1 pound tomatoes, peeled and chopped
1 small tin pimientos, chopped	1 small can pimientos, chopped
2 tablespoons tomato purée	2 tablespoons tomato paste
2 tablespoons molasses	2 tablespoons molasses
1–2 teaspoons dry mustard	1–2 teaspoons dry mustard
1 tablespoon cider vinegar	1 tablespoon cider vinegar
pinch ground cinnamon	pinch ground cinnamon
pinch ground cloves	pinch ground cloves
seasoning to taste	seasoning to taste

1. Drain the beans and cover with fresh water. Bring to a boil and boil for 10 minutes, then cover the saucepan, lower the heat and cook ½ hour.

2. In a clean pan heat the oil and sauté the onions to soften. Mix in the tomatoes, pimientos, tomato purée (paste), molasses, mustard, vinegar, spices and seasoning.

3. Drain and add the beans. Transfer the mixture to an ovenproof casserole and pour in just enough water to cover.

4. Cover the casserole tightly and bake at 300°F/150°C (Gas Mark 2) 3–4 hours or until beans are tender. Stir them every now and again, adding a drop more of the liquid if they seem too dry.

CRÊPES PROVENÇAL

Imperial (Metric)	American
For crêpes:	For crêpes:
4 oz (115g) wholemeal flour	1 cup whole wheat flour
2 oz (55g) soya flour	½ cup soy flour
pinch salt	pinch of salt
1 teaspoon baking powder	1 teaspoon baking powder
½ pint (285ml) water	1⅓ cups water
vegetable oil for frying	vegetable oil for frying
For filling:	For filling:
1 small aubergine	1 small eggplant
1 onion	1 onion
2 courgettes	2 zucchini
3 tablespoons vegetable oil	3 tablespoons vegetable oil
½ lb (225g) tin tomatoes	small can tomatoes
2 tablespoons tomato purée	2 tablespoons tomato purée
½ clove garlic, crushed	½ clove garlic, crushed
½ teaspoon marjoram	½ teaspoon marjoram
seasoning to taste	seasoning to taste
2 oz (55g) peanuts	½ cup peanuts
1 oz (30g) vegan margarine, melted	2½ tablespoons vegan margarine, melted
1 oz (30g) wholemeal breadcrumbs	½ cup whole wheat breadcrumbs
parsley to garnish	parsley to garnish

1. Sieve together the flours, salt and baking powder. Gradually add the water and then beat well to lighten. Refrigerate at least 30 minutes.

2. Cut the aubergine (eggplant) into thick slices and sprinkle with salt. Set aside a short while then rinse with cold water and pat dry.

3. Dice the aubergine; slice the onion and courgettes (zucchini). Heat the oil and add them to the pan, cooking gently until they begin to colour.

4. Drain and chop the tomatoes. Add them to the pan with the purée, garlic, marjoram and seasoning, stirring well. Cover and simmer 5–10 minutes or until all the ingredients are cooked. Add the peanuts.

5. While the vegetables are cooking make the crêpes. The batter will need to be whisked again when taken from the fridge and if it has thickened add a drop more water (it should be the consistency of single—i.e. light—cream).

6. Heat a little oil in a heavy-based pan then pour in just enough batter to cover. Tip the pan to spread it evenly. Cook until the crêpe begins to colour underneath then turn with a spatula (or flip) and quickly cook the other side. Keep cooked crêpes warm while using the rest of the batter in the same way.

7. Fill each one with some of the vegetable mixture, roll up the crêpes and place them neatly side by side in a shallow heatproof dish.

8. Mix the margarine with the breadcrumbs and sprinkle over the crêpes. Put under a medium-hot grill a few minutes to crisp the crumbs. Garnish generously with fresh parsley.

TOFU AND VEGETABLE PAKORA

Imperial (Metric)	American
For batter:	*For batter:*
6 oz (170g) gram (chickpea) flour	**1½ cups gram (chickpea) flour**
1 teaspoon baking powder	**1 teaspoon baking powder**
½ teaspoon ground cumin	**½ teaspoon ground cumin**
½ teaspoon turmeric	**½ teaspoon turmeric**
good pinch cayenne	**good pinch cayenne**
seasoning to taste	**seasoning to taste**
cold water to mix	**cold water to mix**
vegetable oil for frying	**vegetable oil for frying**
For filling:	*For filling:*
½ lb (225g) tofu	**1 cup tofu**
½ small head of broccoli	**½ small head of broccoli**
1 carrot, peeled	**1 carrot, peeled**
1 courgette	**1 zucchini**
8 small mushrooms	**8 small mushrooms**
8 okra	**8 okra**
chutney to serve	**chutney to serve**

1. Sift together the flour, baking powder, spices and seasoning. Add enough water to make a smooth batter—the consistency should be that of a thin white sauce. Beat to lighten then chill the batter.

2. Drain the tofu well, pat dry and cut into cubes. Break the broccoli into fairly large florets; slice the carrot and courgette (zucchini); wipe clean the mushrooms and okra.

3. When ready to prepare the dish beat the batter lightly and adjust the consistency if necessary.

4. Heat a good amount of oil in a deep pan and when it is really hot dip the tofu into the batter (making sure it is well coated) then drop each piece into the oil and deep fry until crisp and golden. Drain on paper towels and keep the tofu warm while cooking the vegetable pieces in the same way.

5. Serve at once with a choice of chutneys. A grain dish and salad would complete the meal.

NOTE: Any vegetables can be used instead of those listed—you need approximately one pound (455g) in total. If not using tofu increase the amount of vegetables. The harder varieties, such as carrots, may need to cook a minute or two longer, though they should still be crisp when served. If you prefer your vegetables well cooked steam them very briefly before dipping into the batter.

CORNISH PASTIES

Imperial (Metric)	American
For pastry:	*For pastry:*
½ lb (225g) wholemeal flour	2 cups whole wheat flour
4 tablespoons vegetable oil	4 tablespoons vegetable oil
good pinch salt	good pinch salt
cold water to mix	cold water to mix
For filling:	*For filling:*
1 potato	1 potato
1 onion	1 onion
1 carrot	1 carrot
½ small parsnip	½ small parsnip
1 stick celery	1 stalk celery
seasoning to taste	seasoning to taste
1 oz (30g) sunflower seeds	1 generous tablespoon sunflower
1 oz (30g) vegan margarine	seeds
	2½ tablespoons vegan margarine

1. Sift the flour into a bowl, add the oil and salt then just enough cold water to make a dough. Wrap this in clingfilm (plastic wrap) and chill 30 minutes.

2. Roll out the dough and cut into 4 circles approximately 5 inches (13cm) in diameter.

3. Peel and dice the potato, onion, carrot and parsnip; chop the celery. Stir the vegetables with the seasoning and sunflower seeds.

4. Spoon a mound of the mixture into the centre of each of the circles of dough. Dot each with some of the margarine. Fold the dough in half to make a traditional pasty shape. Dampen the edges with water and press with a fork to seal them.

5. Transfer the pasties carefully to a lightly greased baking sheet. Bake at 375°F/190°C (Gas Mark 5) 20–30 minutes or until the pastry is crisp and well cooked.

KEBABS

Imperial (Metric)	American
12 small new potatoes, lightly cooked	12 small new potatoes, lightly cooked
8 cherry tomatoes	8 cherry tomatoes
16 button mushrooms	16 button mushrooms
2 small courgettes	2 small zucchini
1 small cauliflower	1 small cauliflower
1 large onion	1 large onion
$\frac{1}{2}$ lb (225g) tofu	1 cup tofu
bay leaves	bay leaves
For dressing:	*For dressing:*
$\frac{1}{4}$ pint (140ml) vegetable oil	$\frac{2}{3}$ cup vegetable oil
3 tablespoons wine vinegar	3 tablespoons wine vinegar
$\frac{1}{2}$ teaspoon dried marjoram	$\frac{1}{2}$ teaspoon dried marjoram
$\frac{1}{2}$ teaspoon dried basil	$\frac{1}{2}$ teaspoon dried basil
$\frac{1}{2}$ teaspoon dried oregano	$\frac{1}{2}$ teaspoon dried oregano
generous pinch garlic salt	generous pinch garlic salt
fresh ground pepper	fresh ground pepper

1. Dry the potatoes, wash and dry the tomatoes and mushrooms. Cut the courgettes (zucchini) into 1 inch (2.5cm) slices. Break the cauliflower into large florets. Peel the onion, cut into thick wedges and separate the layers to divide each wedge into 2 or 3 pieces.

2. Drain the tofu well and cut into even-sized cubes.

3. Halve the potatoes, then alternate them on 8 or 12 skewers (depending on size) with all the other ingredients, arranging them to look attractive.

4. Put the ingredients for the dressing into a screwtop jar and shake to mix.

5. Lay the skewers on a baking sheet and brush the kebabs generously with the dressing. Grill under medium heat, turning frequently, and brushing each time with more of the dressing.

6. The kebabs will be ready to serve when the ingredients begin to colour and are becoming tender. This will take about 10 minutes. Make sure they are piping hot. Serve with fresh-from-the-oven bread or on a bed of rice.

OVEN FARE

CHINESE CABBAGE ROLLS

Imperial (Metric)	American
1 large Chinese cabbage	1 large Chinese cabbage
2 tablespoons vegetable oil	2 tablespoons vegetable oil
2 spring onions, chopped	2 scallions, chopped
4 oz (115g) mushrooms, sliced	2 cups mushrooms, sliced
4 oz (115g) mange tout	¼ pound snow peas
2 oz (55g) cashew nut pieces	½ cup cashew nut pieces
4 oz (115g) beansprouts	2 cups beansprouts
soya sauce	soy sauce
seasoning to taste	seasoning to taste
2 oz (55g) cooked millet or other grain	⅓ cup cooked millet or other grain
⅓ pint (200ml) vegetable stock	¾ cup vegetable stock

1. Break 8 large leaves off the Chinese cabbage. Blanch them a few minutes in a large pan of boiling water then drain well and lay them flat on a board. Set aside.

2. Heat the oil, add the spring onions (scallions) and cook a few minutes. Add the mushrooms, stir and cook a few minutes more.

3. Top, tail and wash the mange tout (snow peas) and if necessary, trim the sides. Add them whole to the pan with the cashew pieces. Continue cooking 2 minutes then add the beansprouts, soya sauce, seasoning and cooked millet.

4. Place a spoonful or two of the mixture onto each leaf and roll it up carefully, turning in the top and bottom to make an oblong package. Arrange side by side in a shallow ovenproof dish.

5. Pour in the stock, cover the dish with a lid or foil and bake at 350°F/180°C (Gas Mark 4) 30 minutes. Serve at once.

Pizza

Imperial (Metric)	American
For base:	*For dough:*
½ teaspoon dried yeast	½ teaspoon dried yeast
¼ pint (140ml) warm water	⅔ cup warm water
½ lb (225g) wholemeal flour	2 cups whole wheat flour
1 tablespoon vegetable oil	1 tablespoon vegetable oil
2 teaspoons dry basil	2 teaspoons dry basil
seasoning to taste	seasoning to taste
For topping:	*For topping:*
Tomato sauce (see page 82)	Tomato sauce (see page 82)
3 oz (85g) cooked sweetcorn, drained	½ cup cooked corn, drained
1 green pepper, cut in thin rings	1 green pepper, cut in thin rings
4 oz (115g) mushrooms, sliced	2 cups mushrooms, sliced
small tin artichoke hearts, drained	small can artichoke hearts, drained
2 oz (55g) pine nuts	½ cup pine nuts
1–2 teaspoons oregano	1–2 teaspoons oregano
seasoning to taste	seasoning to taste
approximately 2 tablespoons vegetable oil	approximately 2 tablespoons vegetable oil
black olives to garnish	black olives to garnish

1. Mix the yeast with the warm water then stir until it dissolves. Set aside in a warm spot until the mixture begins to froth.

2. Put the flour into a warmed bowl, add the yeast liquid and mix to make a dough. Add the oil, basil and seasoning. On a floured board knead the dough 5 minutes.

3. Cover the bowl containing the kneaded dough and leave it in a warm spot until the dough doubles in size.

4. Knock back (punch down) the dough. Divide it into 4 even-sized pieces and roll them out to make thin circles. Place these on lightly greased baking sheets and leave in a warm spot 20 minutes.

5. When ready to cook the pizzas, spread each one with tomato sauce. Sprinkle with the corn, top with the pepper rings then the mushrooms and artichoke hearts.

6. Sprinkle with pine nuts, oregano and seasoning. Trickle a little oil over the top of each pizza. Decorate with black olives.

7. Bake at 400°F/200°C (Gas Mark 6) 20 minutes, or until the dough is cooked and the vegetables tender.

NOTE: This method makes a thick pizza. For a crisper base do not set the dough aside to rise. Simple knead it well, divide into 4, add the topping and cook at once. If liked, you can bake the dough 5 minutes at the same temperature before adding the topping. This ensures a less soggy base.

REFRIED BEAN ENCHILADAS

Imperial (Metric)
For tortillas:
6 oz (170g) maize flour
pinch salt
approximately ⅓ pint (200ml)
warm water
vegetable oil for frying
For filling:
½ lb (225g) kidney beans, soaked
overnight
2 oz (55g) vegan margarine
1 large onion, chopped
1–2 cloves garlic, crushed
3 tablespoons tomato purée
good pinch chilli powder
1 teaspoon oregano
1 bay leaf
seasoning to taste
⅓ pint (200ml) undiluted soya milk
1 teaspoon arrowroot
2 tablespoons cold water
paprika and raw onion rings to
garnish

American
For tortillas:
1½ cups cornmeal
pinch salt
¾ cup warm water
vegetable oil for frying
For filling:
1 cup kidney beans, soaked
overnight
¼ cup vegan margarine
1 large onion, chopped
1–2 cloves garlic, crushed
3 tablespoons tomato paste
good pinch chili powder
1 teaspoon oregano
1 bay leaf
seasoning to taste
¾ cup undiluted soy milk
1 teaspoon arrowroot
2 tablespoons cold water
paprika and raw onion rings to
garnish

1. To make the tortillas sift together the maize flour (cornmeal) and salt, then gradually stir in enough water to bind to a fairly soft dough. Divide into 8 equal-sized portions and roll out between clingfilm (plastic wrap) to make very thin circles. Set aside.

2. Put the beans in a saucepan with fresh water and boil 10 minutes. Lower the heat, cover the pan and cook 1½—2 hours or until the beans are soft, adding more water as necessary.

3. Melt the margarine and sauté the onion and garlic, stirring frequently. When cooked but not browned add the tomato purée (paste), chilli powder, oregano, bay leaf and seasoning. Drain the beans, mash them and stir them into the mixture. Cook gently 5 minutes more, taking care it does not dry out.

4. Cook the tortillas one at a time in a lightly oiled heavy-based frying pan. They should need only a few minutes on each side to colour. Add more oil as necessary.

5. Spread the bean mixture over the tortillas and fold them loosely. Place them close together, flap side down, in a shallow ovenproof dish and keep them warm.

6. Put the soya milk into a small saucepan and stir in the arrowroot mixed with the water. Heat gently, stirring continually, so that it thickens. Pour the sauce over the enchiladas and pop the dish under a grill for a few minutes.

7. Serve topped with a sprinkling of paprika and raw onion rings.

NOTE: Although the name of this dish gives the impression the beans are twice fried, it actually refers to the fact that they are cooked twice—boiled and then fried. The mixture makes a good filling, too, for ordinary pancakes, pasties, lasagne and so on.

ALMOND-RICE STUFFED PEPPERS

Imperial (Metric)	American
2 large green peppers	2 large green peppers
1 large red pepper	1 large red pepper
1 large yellow pepper	1 large yellow pepper
approximately 4 tablespoons vegetable oil	approximately 4 tablespoons vegetable oil
1 onion, chopped	1 onion, chopped
2 sticks celery, finely chopped	2 stalks celery, finely chopped
6 oz (170g) brown rice	¾ cup brown rice
¾ (425ml) vegetable stock or water	2 cups vegetable stock or water
1 teaspoon basil	1 teaspoon basil
1 teaspoon oregano	1 teaspoon oregano
2 tablespoons cooked peas	2 tablespoons cooked peas
seasoning to taste	seasoning to taste
2 oz (55g) almonds, coarsely chopped	½ cup almonds, coarsely chopped
2 tablespoons chopped parsley	2 tablespoons chopped parsley

1. Blanch the peppers 5 minutes in a large pan of boiling water. Drain then rinse them in cold water and drain well again. Cut into even-sized halves and stand these close together in a shallow ovenproof dish.

2. Heat 2 tablespoons of oil in a large pan and sauté the onion a few minutes. Add the celery and cook a few minutes more then stir in the rice.

3. Add the vegetable stock, bring to a boil then cover the pan and simmer the rice 20 minutes or until just cooked. Add the herbs, peas and seasoning and cook a little longer uncovered so that the rice is fairly dry. (Drain if necessary.)

4. Meanwhile heat 1 tablespoon of oil and sauté the nuts until crisp and golden. Stir them into the rice with the parsley.

5. Use this mixture to fill the pepper shells, piling it high if necessary. Trickle a little more oil over the top of each one.

6. Cover with a lid or foil and bake at 350°F/180°C (Gas Mark 4) 20–30 minutes.

Butter (Lima) Bean Pie

Imperial (Metric)	American
For pastry:	*For pastry:*
4 oz (115g) wholemeal flour	**1 cup whole wheat flour**
2 tablespoons vegetable oil	**2 tablespoons vegetable oil**
pinch of salt	**pinch of salt**
approximately 4 tablespoons cold water	**approximately 4 tablespoons cold water**
½ oz (15g) sesame seeds	**1 generous tablespoon sesame seeds**
For filling:	*For filling:*
4 oz (115g) butter beans, soaked overnight	**⅔ cup lima beans, soaked overnight**
½ small cauliflower	**½ small cauliflower**
2 tablespoons vegetable oil	**2 tablespoons vegetable oil**
1 small onion, sliced	**1 small onion, sliced**
1 oz (30g) wholemeal flour	**¼ cup whole wheat flour**
seasoning to taste	**seasoning to taste**
parsley to garnish	**parsley to garnish**

1. Sift the flour, stir in the oil and salt. Gradually add cold water to make a soft dough. Sprinkle with the seeds. Knead briefly. Cover with clingfilm (plastic wrap) and chill 30 minutes.

2. Meanwhile put the beans in a pan with fresh water and boil 10 minutes. Lower the heat and simmer about 1 hour or until just cooked.

3. Trim the cauliflower and cut into florets. Cook in boiling water until tender. Drain well, reserving the water.

4. Heat the oil in a clean pan and sauté the onion until it begins to colour. Sprinkle in the flour, stir and cook a few minutes. Pour in about ½ pint (285ml or 1⅓ cups) of the cauliflower water, bring to a boil then simmer to make a thick sauce. Season to taste.

5. Stir the cauliflower and beans into the sauce then spoon the mixture into a small ovenproof dish.

6. Roll out the pastry as thin as you can, lift carefully and place on top of the beans. Dampen the edges and seal well. Use a fork to prick a pattern in the top.

7. Bake at 400°F/200°C (Gas Mark 6) 20 minutes or until the pastry is crisp and beginning to colour. Serve at once garnished with parsley.

Tofu Layered Casserole

Imperial (Metric)	American
1 lb (455g) potatoes	1 pound potatoes
1 small head of broccoli	1 small head of broccoli
2 tablespoons vegetable oil	2 tablespoons vegetable oil
1 onion, thickly sliced	1 onion, thickly sliced
1 clove garlic, crushed	1 clove garlic, crushed
4 oz (115g) mushrooms, sliced	2 cups mushrooms, sliced
6 oz (170g) tofu, well drained and cubed	¾ cup tofu, well drained and cubed
1 tablespoon parsley	1 tablespoon parsley
seasoning to taste	seasoning to taste
1 oz (30g) vegan margarine	2½ tablespoons vegan margarine
1 oz (30g) peanuts, coarsely chopped	¼ cup peanuts, coarsely chopped
1 oz (30g) wholemeal breadcrumbs	½ cup whole wheat breadcrumbs
parsley to garnish	parsley to garnish

1. Scrub the potatoes then steam them until half cooked. Drain well. When cool enough to handle, cut into thin slices.

2. Trim the broccoli into florets. Steam them 5 minutes only then drain.

3. Heat the oil in a heavy-based pan and sauté the onion and the garlic. When soft, add the mushrooms and the broccoli. Stir, then cook gently 5 minutes more.

4. Remove the vegetables from the pan, add a drop more oil if necessary and briefly sauté the tofu to colour.

5. Mix the vegetables with the tofu, parsley and seasoning.

6. In a greased casserole lay one third of the potatoes across the base. Spoon in half of the vegetable and tofu mixture. Repeat this then top with remaining potato slices.

7. Melt the margarine in a clean pan and briefly sauté the peanuts and the breadcrumbs. Sprinkle this mixture over the top of the casserole together with any fat that remains in the pan (add a knob or two more of margarine if necessary).

8. Bake uncovered at 350°F/180°C (Gas Mark 4) 30 minutes. Garnish with parsley.

ADUKI BEAN AND LEEK PASTIES

Imperial (Metric)	American
For pastry:	*For pastry:*
6 oz (170g) wholemeal flour	1½ cups whole wheat flour
salt	salt
3 oz (85g) vegan margarine	⅓ cup vegan margarine
approximately 3 tablespoons cold water	approximately 3 tablespoons cold water
For filling:	*For filling:*
4 oz (115g) aduki beans, soaked overnight	½ cup aduki beans, soaked overnight
2 tablespoons vegetable oil	2 tablespoons vegetable oil
1 onion, peeled and finely chopped	1 onion, peeled and finely chopped
1 leek, trimmed, washed and finely chopped	1 leek, trimmed, washed and finely chopped
1 carrot, scrubbed and finely chopped	1 carrot, scrubbed and finely chopped
½ lb (225g) tin tomatoes, drained	small can tomatoes, drained
½ teaspoon dried rosemary	½ teaspoon dried rosemary
soya sauce	soy sauce
seasoning to taste	seasoning to taste

1. Sift the flour into a bowl with the salt. Use fingertips to rub in the margarine to make a crumb-like mixture then add cold water to bind it to a dough. Wrap in clingfilm (plastic wrap) and refrigerate 30 minutes.

2. Put the aduki beans in fresh water, boil 10 minutes then cover the saucepan and simmer the beans 1 hour or until very soft. Drain well.

3. Heat the oil and sauté the onion, leek and carrot. When they begin to colour stir in the tomatoes, chop coarsely, and add the herbs. Cook over medium heat until the mixture begins to thicken.

4. Add soya sauce and seasoning to taste. Mash the beans and stir these into the vegetables.

5. Roll out the pastry and cut into 4 large circles. Spread some of the mixture on half of each one. Fold the remaining dough over to make a pasty and dampen the edges; crimp to seal. Prick each pasty a few times with a fork.

6. Place them carefully on a lightly greased baking sheet. Bake at 400°F/200°C (Gas Mark 6) 20 minutes or until the pastry is cooked.

CORN AND TOMATO LASAGNE

Imperial (Metric)	American
8 sheets spinach lasagne	8 sheets spinach lasagne
10 oz (285g) sweetcorn kernels, fresh or frozen	1⅔ cups corn kernels, fresh or frozen
3 tablespoons vegetable oil	3 tablespoons vegetable oil
1 small green pepper, chopped	1 small green pepper, chopped
1 small onion, chopped	1 small onion, chopped
1 lb (455g) tomatoes	1 pound tomatoes
⅓ pint (200ml) vegetable stock	¾ cup vegetable stock
½–1 teaspoon mixed herbs	½–1 teaspoon mixed herbs
1 tablespoon tomato purée	1 tablespoon tomato paste
1 tablespoon red wine	1 tablespoon red wine
seasoning to taste	seasoning to taste
1 oz (30g) wholemeal flour	¼ cup whole wheat flour
½ pint (285ml) soya milk	1⅓ cups soy milk
2 tablespoons chopped parsley	2 tablespoons chopped parsley
1 oz (30g) wholemeal breadcrumbs	½ cup whole wheat breadcrumbs

1. Cook the lasagne in a pan of boiling salted water 6–8 minutes or until just tender. Lay the sheets on clean tea or dish towels, making sure sheets do not touch. Set aside.

2. Cook the corn and drain well. Set aside.

3. Heat 2 tablespoons of the oil and sauté the pepper and onion 5 minutes. Coarsely chop and add the tomatoes, vegetable stock, herbs, tomato purée (paste), wine and seasoning. Bring to a boil, cover and simmer 20 minutes.

4. Meanwhile make a parsley sauce by heating the remaining tablespoon of oil in a pan and cooking the flour briefly. Stir in the milk, bring to a boil then simmer until the sauce thickens. Add the parsley and seasoning to taste.

5. Lightly grease a shallow tin or dish then lay about one third of the lasagne across the base. Top with half the tomato sauce, then half the corn. Repeat this process. Finish with the remaining lasagne and cover with the white sauce, tipping the container so that it is evenly distributed. Sprinkle with breadcrumbs.

6. Bake at 375°F/190°C (Gas Mark 5) 20–30 minutes or until the top is crisp.

Cassoulet

Imperial (Metric)	American
6 oz (170g) black-eyed peas, soaked overnight	1 cup black-eyed peas, soaked overnight
14 oz (395g) tin tomatoes	medium can tomatoes
⅓ pint (200ml) vegetable stock	¾ cup vegetable stock
½ clove garlic, crushed	½ clove garlic, crushed
seasoning to taste	seasoning to taste
2 leeks	2 leeks
1 small cauliflower	1 small cauliflower
medium tin soya or nut "sausage"	medium can soy or nut "sausage"
2 oz (55g) wholemeal breadcrumbs	1 cup whole wheat breadcrumbs

1. Drain the beans and put them into a saucepan with the tomatoes, vegetable stock, garlic and seasoning.

2. Bring to a boil and continue boiling 10 minutes then transfer the mixture to a casserole; cover and bake at 300°F/150°C (Gas Mark 2) 1 hour.

3. Clean, trim and chop the leeks; divide the cauliflower into florets; drain the "sausages" and cut them into pieces. Stir these into the bean mixture.

4. Cover the top with the breadcrumbs and bake, uncovered, at the same temperature a further hour or until all the ingredients are cooked.

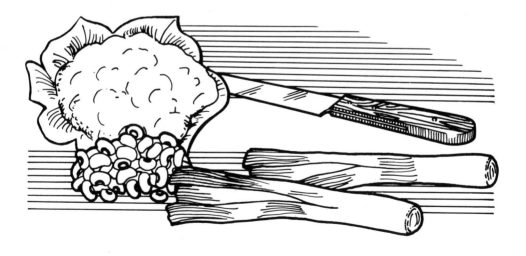

PARSNIP SHEPHERD'S PIE

Imperial (Metric)	American
½ lb (225g) lentils, soaked overnight	1 cup lentils, soaked overnight
1 tablespoon vegetable oil	1 tablespoon vegetable oil
1 onion, finely chopped	1 onion, finely chopped
1 stick celery, chopped	1 stalk celery, chopped
1 teaspoon thyme	1 teaspoon thyme
seasoning to taste	seasoning to taste
2 large parsnips	2 large parsnips
pinch nutmeg	pinch nutmeg
1 oz (30g) vegan margarine	2½ tablespoons vegan margarine
1-2 tablespoons undiluted soya milk	1-2 tablespoons undiluted soy milk

1. Put the lentils into a saucepan with fresh water, bring to a boil and continue boiling 10 minutes. Lower the heat and simmer 45 minutes.

2. Heat the oil and sauté the onion a few minutes. Add the celery and cook 5 minutes more. Stir in the thyme and seasoning. Drain and stir in the lentils. Transfer the mixture to an ovenproof dish.

3. Peel and chop the parsnips. Steam or boil them until very tender. Drain well, then mash together with the nutmeg, margarine and soya milk, making sure the purée is completely smooth. Add seasoning. Spread the purée over the lentil mixture and level the top.

4. Bake at 375°F/190°C (Gas Mark 5) 20 minutes. Serve hot.

CELERY CRUMBLE

Imperial (Metric)	American
1 small head celery	1 small head celery
2 carrots	2 carrots
2 tablespoons vegetable oil	2 tablespoons vegetable oil
1 oz (30g) wholemeal flour	$\frac{1}{4}$ cup whole wheat flour
$\frac{1}{2}$ pint (285ml) soya milk	$1\frac{1}{3}$ cups soy milk
chopped parsley	chopped parsley
seasoning to taste	seasoning to taste
3 oz (85g) walnuts	$\frac{3}{4}$ cup walnuts
For crumble:	*For crumble:*
2 oz (55g) wholemeal flour	$\frac{1}{2}$ cup whole wheat flour
2 oz (55g) oats	$\frac{1}{2}$ cup oats
2 oz (55g) vegan margarine	$\frac{1}{4}$ cup vegan margarine
seasoning to taste	seasoning to taste

1. Trim the celery then cut into even-sized pieces. Slice the carrots. Steam the vegetables 10 minutes or until beginning to soften.

2. Heat the oil in a separate pan, sprinkle in the flour, cook briefly. Add the milk and bring to a boil then simmer to make a sauce. Stir in the chopped parsley and seasoning.

3. Drain and add the vegetables and the walnuts. Transfer the mixture to an ovenproof dish.

4. Make a crumble by stirring together the flour and oats then rubbing in the margarine with your fingertips. Season to taste. Sprinkle the crumble evenly over the celery mixture.

5. Bake at 400°F/200°C (Gas Mark 6) 20–30 minutes or until crisp and brown.

ONION DUMPLINGS

Imperial (Metric)	American
4 large onions	**4 large onions**
For pastry:	*For pastry:*
10 oz (285g) wholemeal flour	**2½ cups whole wheat flour**
pinch salt	**pinch salt**
5 oz (140g) vegan margarine	**scant ⅔ cup vegan margarine**
approximately 3 tablespoons cold water	**approximately 3 tablespoons cold water**
For filling:	*For filling:*
3 tablespoons vegetable oil	**3 tablespoons vegetable oil**
2 oz (55g) kasha (roasted buckwheat)	**¼ cup kasha (roasted buckwheat)**
1 bay leaf	**1 bay leaf**
approximately ⅓ pint (200ml) boiling water	**¾ cup boiling water**
½ red pepper, diced	**½ red pepper, diced**
small chunk white cabbage, finely shredded	**small chunk white cabbage, finely shredded**
2 oz (55g) peanuts, coarsely chopped	**½ cup peanuts, coarsely chopped**
1 teaspoon tarragon	**1 teaspoon tarragon**
soya sauce	**soy sauce**
seasoning to taste	**seasoning to taste**

1. Peel the onions and cut a slice from the bottom of each so that they stand firm. Carefully remove the inner flesh leaving a shell about 3 layers thick. Blanch the shells in a pan of salted boiling water a few minutes then drain well. Chop the centres and reserve.

2. Make the pastry next. Sift together the flour and salt, rub in the margarine to make a crumb-like mixture and add enough water to bind it so that you have a soft, pliable dough. Wrap in clingfilm (plastic wrap) and chill briefly.

3. Heat 1 tablespoon oil and gently sauté the kasha a few minutes. Add the bay leaf, pour in the water, bring to a boil then lower the heat and cook 20 minutes. Drain off any excess water. Remove the bay leaf.

4. In a clean pan heat the remaining oil and sauté the onion centres and red pepper a few minutes. Add the cabbage and peanuts and cook 5 minutes more, stirring occasionally. Add the kasha, herbs, soya sauce and seasoning to taste. Mix well.

5. Roll out the pastry and cut it into 4 large squares. Stand an onion shell on each one and use the kasha mixture to fill them to the top. Carefully lift up the dough and wrap it around the onions, dampening the edges and pressing to seal.

6. Transfer the dumplings to a baking sheet. Bake at 375°F/190°C (Gas Mark 5) 20–30 minutes or until the pastry is cooked. Serve hot.

TOMATO FLAN WITH TOFU

Imperial (Metric)	American
For pastry:	*For pastry:*
6 oz (170g) wholemeal flour	1½ cups whole wheat flour
pinch salt	pinch salt
1 teaspoon baking powder	1 teaspoon baking powder
3 oz (85g) vegan margarine	⅓ cup vegan margarine
approximately 3 tablespoons cold water	approximately 3 tablespoons cold water
1 teaspoon mixed herbs	1 teaspoon mixed herbs
For filling:	*For filling:*
1 tablespoon vegetable oil	1 tablespoon vegetable oil
1 onion, sliced	1 onion, sliced
1 green pepper, sliced	1 green pepper, sliced
½ lb (225g) tomatoes	½ pound tomatoes
½ lb (225g) tofu	1 cup tofu
cold water to mix	cold water to mix
seasoning to taste	seasoning to taste
pinch chilli powder	pinch of chili powder
watercress to garnish	watercress to garnish

1. Sift together the flour, salt and baking powder. Rub in the margarine to make a mixture like breadcrumbs then add just enough water to make a dough. Sprinkle with herbs. Wrap in clingfilm (plastic wrap) and chill.

2. Heat the oil in a pan and sauté the onion and pepper until they are soft but not brown. Drain well on paper towels.

3. Roll out the pastry and use it to line a medium-sized flan dish. Spread the onion-and-pepper mixture across the base. Slice the tomatoes and arrange on top.

4. Drain the tofu, mash well and mix with just enough water to make a thick creamy sauce. (If you have a blender, use this for a smoother sauce.) Add plenty of seasoning and a pinch of chilli powder.

5. Pour the sauce carefully over the vegetables. Bake at 375°F/190°C (Gas Mark 5) 20–30 minutes or until the pastry is crisp. Garnish with sprigs of watercress before serving.

STUFFED MARROW (SUMMER SQUASH) RINGS

Imperial (Metric)	American
1 medium marrow	1 medium summer squash
2 tablespoons vegetable oil	2 tablespoons vegetable oil
1 onion, chopped	1 onion, chopped
5 oz (140g) soya "mince," hydrated in water	1¼ cups soy "mince," hydrated in water
1 carrot, finely sliced	1 carrot, finely sliced
1 stick celery, finely sliced	1 stalk celery, finely sliced
1 teaspoon thyme	1 teaspoon thyme
seasoning to taste	seasoning to taste
1 oz (30g) wholemeal flour	¼ cup whole wheat flour
½ pint (285ml) vegetable stock	1⅓ cups vegetable stock
tomato sauce to serve (see page 82)	tomato sauce to serve (see page 82)

1. Peel the marrow (squash) and cut into 4 thick slices (about 2 inches or 5 cm). Remove the seeds, and a little of the flesh if the centre hole is small. Place the rings close together in a greased, shallow ovenproof dish.

2. Heat the oil and sauté the onion a few minutes. Drain the soya "mince" and add to the pan, cooking gently 5 minutes more.

3. Add the carrot and celery, thyme and seasoning. Stir in the flour and cook a minute. Add the vegetable stock. Cook gently 15–20 minutes, stirring occasionally, until all the ingredients are just cooked.

4. Spoon the mixture into the marrow rings, piling it up if necessary. Cover the dish with a lid or foil.

5. Bake at 350°F/180°C (Gas Mark 4) 20–30 minutes or until cooked. Serve with hot tomato sauce.

FOIL-BAKED JACKET POTATOES

Imperial (Metric)	*American*
4 large potatoes	**4 large potatoes**
vegetable oil	**vegetable oil**
Filling 1:	*Filling 1:*
2 tomatoes	**2 tomatoes**
2 spring onions	**2 scallions**
black olives, pitted	**black olives, pitted**
capers, according to taste	**capers, according to taste**
little lemon juice	**little lemon juice**
little olive oil	**little olive oil**
seasoning	**seasoning**
2 oz (55g) tofu, well drained	**¼ cup tofu, well drained**
Filling 2:	*Filling 2:*
2 tablespoons vegetable oil	**2 tablespoons vegetable oil**
2 courgettes, chopped	**2 zucchini, chopped**
1 oz (30g) peanuts, chopped	**¼ cup peanuts, chopped**
½ oz (15g) sesame seeds	**1 tablespoon sesame seeds**
Filling 3:	*Filling 3:*
1 large ripe avocado	**1 large ripe avocado**
¼ small onion, finely chopped	**¼ small onion, finely chopped**
pinch of chilli powder	**pinch of chili powder**
approximately 3 tablespoons soya mayonnaise	**approximately 3 tablespoons soy mayonnaise**
Filling 4:	*Filling 4:*
4 oz (115g) mushrooms	**2 cups mushrooms**
1 tablespoon vegetable oil	**1 tablespoon vegetable oil**
2 tablespoons cooked sweetcorn, drained	**2 tablespoons cooked corn, drained**
1 oz (30g) roasted sunflower seeds	**¼ cup roasted sunflower seeds**
soya sauce	**soy sauce**

1. Scrub the potatoes well then dry them. Rub the skins with a little oil. Wrap each one in a piece of foil. Bake at 400°F/200°C (Gas Mark 6) 1–1½ hours or until they give when pressed.

2. Either use just one of the suggested fillings (increasing the amount accordingly), or serve a selection of toppings in separate dishes.

3. For Filling 1: Coarsely chop the tomatoes, finely chop the spring onions (scallions) and halve the olives. Mix well with the capers, lemon juice, oil and seasoning. Add the tofu, diced or mashed.

4. For Filling 2: Heat the oil and sauté the courgettes (zucchini), stirring occasionally, 10 minutes. Add the peanuts and the seeds and cook 5 minutes more or until the courgettes begin to colour. Season to taste.

5. For Filling 3: Mash the avocado with the onion, chilli powder and enough mayonnaise to make a thick, creamy mixture.

6. For Filling 4: Slice the mushrooms and sauté them in oil until just tender. Stir in the corn and cook briefly. Add the seeds and sauce to taste.

PEPPER RAGOUT

Imperial (Metric)	American
2–3 tablespoons vegetable oil	2–3 tablespoons vegetable oil
2 red peppers, thickly sliced	2 red peppers, thickly sliced
2 green peppers, thickly sliced	2 green peppers, thickly sliced
1 onion, thickly sliced	1 onion, thickly sliced
1 clove garlic, crushed	1 clove garlic, crushed
2 sticks celery, chopped	2 stalks celery, chopped
4 oz (115g) cooked chickpeas, drained	½ cup cooked chickpeas, drained
¼ pint (140ml) vegetable stock	⅔ cup vegetable stock
seasoning to taste	seasoning to taste
1 teaspoon marjoram	1 teaspoon marjoram
½ oz (15g) wholemeal flour	2 tablespoons whole wheat flour
1 tablespoon cold water	1 tablespoon cold water
3 tablespoons undiluted soya milk or tahini	3 tablespoons undiluted soy milk or tahini

1. Heat the oil and gently sauté the peppers and onion with the garlic and celery. Stir occasionally.

2. When beginning to colour, add the chickpeas, vegetable stock, seasoning and marjoram. Transfer to an ovenproof dish, cover and bake at 350°F/180°C (Gas Mark 4) 30 minutes. Add a drop more liquid if necessary.

3. Mix the flour with a little water and stir into the other ingredients. Cook uncovered 10 minutes or so more. When the liquid thickens and the vegetables are cooked remove the dish from the heat and stir in the milk or tahini to give the ragout a creamy texture.

CHICORY (ENDIVE) À LA CRÈME

Imperial (Metric)	American
4 heads chicory	**4 heads endive**
1 large red pepper	**1 large red pepper**
¼ pint (140ml) vegetable stock	**⅔ cup vegetable stock**
squeeze lemon juice	**squeeze lemon juice**
seasoning to taste	**seasoning to taste**
pinch nutmeg	**pinch nutmeg**
¼ pint (140ml) undiluted soya milk	**⅔ cup undiluted soy milk**
1 teaspoon arrowroot	**1 teaspoon arrowroot**
1 tablespoon cold water	**1 tablespoon cold water**
1 teaspoon mixed herbs	**1 teaspoon mixed herbs**
soya "bacon" bits or soya nuts (see below) to garnish	**soy "bacon" bits or soy nuts (see below) to garnish**
bulgur to serve	**bulgur to serve**

1. Trim the heads of chicory (endive) and the pepper. Blanch them in a pan of boiling water 5 minutes. Cool, then cut the chicory across into thick slices and the pepper into thin rings.

2. In a greased, shallow ovenproof dish, layer the chicory and pepper rings until all have been used. Mix the vegetable stock with the lemon juice, seasoning and nutmeg and pour over the vegetables. Cover the dish and bake at 325°F/170°C (Gas Mark 3) ½ hour or until the vegetables are cooked.

3. Put the soya milk into a small saucepan. Mix the arrowroot with the water to make a smooth paste and add it to the pan. Heat gently, stirring, until the mixture thickens. Add herbs and seasoning. Pour the cream sauce over the vegetables and put under a grill briefly to heat through.

4. Serve at once with a sprinkling of soya "bacon" bits or soya nuts to add a crisp contrast. A base of bulgur (one of the more delicately flavoured grains) would go well.

* To make soya nuts, first soak the soya beans overnight (or in boiling water 1 hour). They must then be dried thoroughly and deep fried in hot oil 10–15 minutes or until light gold in colour. Drain on paper towels, sprinkle with salt, leave to cool. If using them with the above recipe you might prefer to oven-bake the beans at the same time. Soak them, boil 1 hour, then dry well and lay them on a baking sheet, turning occasionally. They should be ready in approximately 30 minutes.

"PORK" AND PASTA BAKE

Imperial (Metric)	American
5 oz (140g) soya "pork" chunks, hydrated in water	5 ounces soy "pork" chunks, hydrated in water
3 tablespoons vegetable oil	3 tablespoons vegetable oil
1 small onion, sliced	1 small onion, sliced
1 red pepper, sliced	1 red pepper, sliced
1 oz (30g) wholemeal flour	$\frac{1}{4}$ cup whole wheat flour
1 generous teaspoon ground ginger	1 generous teaspoon ground ginger
$\frac{1}{2}$ pint (285ml) vegetable stock	1$\frac{1}{3}$ cups vegetable stock
$\frac{1}{4}$ pint (140ml) cider	$\frac{2}{3}$ cup cider
2 tablespoons wine vinegar	2 tablespoons wine vinegar
1 teaspoon raw cane sugar	1 teaspoon raw cane sugar
soya sauce	soy sauce
$\frac{1}{2}$ lb (225g) tin pineapple chunks in natural juice	small can pineapple chunks in natural juice
4 oz (115g) wholemeal pasta shells	2 cups whole wheat pasta shells

1. Drain the soya chunks well. Heat 2 tablespoons oil and sauté the cubes, stirring frequently, a few minutes. Remove them from the pan.

2. Add the remaining oil and sauté the onion and pepper until beginning to soften. Stir in the flour and ginger and cook a minute or two more.

3. Add the vegetable stock and cider, the vinegar, sugar and soya sauce. Return the soya chunks to the mixture, stir well, cook briefly and then transfer to a casserole.

4. Cover with a lid or foil and bake at 300°F/150°C (Gas Mark 2) 30 minutes.

5. Add the drained pineapple chunks and the pasta. (If the sauce is very thick, stir in a little of the juice—otherwise, reserve it for use in another recipe.)

6. Cover the casserole and continue cooking a further 30 minutes or until all the ingredients are tender.

CARROT AND TURNIP FLAN

Imperial (Metric)	American
For pastry:	*For pastry:*
6 oz (170g) oats	**1½ cups oats**
3 oz (85g) vegan margarine	**⅓ cup vegan margarine**
seasoning to taste	**seasoning to taste**
1 oz (30g) sunflower seeds, coarsely crushed	**1 generous tablespoon sunflower seeds, coarsely crushed**
For filling:	*For filling:*
1¼ lb (565g) carrots	**1¼ pounds carrots**
¾ lb (340g) turnips	**¾ pound turnips**
1 oz (30g) vegan margarine	**2½ tablespoons vegan margarine**
2 tablespoons wholemeal flour	**2 tablespoons whole wheat flour**
⅓ pint (200ml) soya milk	**¾ cup soy milk**
seasoning to taste	**seasoning to taste**
¼ teaspoon ground ginger	**¼ teaspoon ground ginger**
parsley to garnish	**parsley to garnish**

1. Put the oats into a bowl and rub in the margarine. Add seasoning and sunflower seeds, mixing so that they are well distributed. Press the crumb-like mixture into a medium-sized greased flan dish, making sure it is spread evenly. Set aside.

2. Peel, cube and steam the carrots and turnips until tender. Drain and mash or blend to a purée.

3. Melt the margarine in a clean pan and gently cook the wholemeal flour a minute. Stir in the milk and simmer to thicken.

4. Combine the sauce with the vegetable purée. Add seasoning and ginger. Spoon the mixture into the prepared flan case and smooth the top.

5. Bake at 400°F/200°C (Gas Mark 6) 15 minutes or until cooked.

AUBERGINE (EGGPLANT) PROVENÇAL WITH TAHINI SAUCE

Imperial (Metric)	American
2 aubergines	2 eggplants
salt	salt
4 tablespoons vegetable oil	4 tablespoons vegetable oil
1 onion, sliced	1 onion, sliced
1 clove garlic, crushed	1 clove garlic, crushed
1 lb (455g) tomatoes	1 pound tomatoes
seasoning to taste	seasoning to taste
1 tablespoon chopped parsley	1 tablespoon chopped parsley
4 oz (115g) cooked peas, drained	¾ cup cooked peas, drained
2 oz (55g) wholemeal breadcrumbs	1 cup whole wheat breadcrumbs
1 oz (30g) sesame seeds	¼ cup sesame seeds
For sauce:	*For sauce:*
1 tablespoon vegetable oil	1 tablespoon vegetable oil
1 oz (30g) wholemeal flour	¼ cup whole wheat flour
½ pint (285ml) water	1⅓ cups water
approximately 2 tablespoons tahini	approximately 2 tablespoons tahini

1. Wash the aubergines (eggplants) and cut them into thick slices, sprinkle with salt and set aside 30 minutes. Rinse with cold water and dry carefully.

2. Heat half the oil and sauté the onion and garlic 5 minutes. Cut the aubergine into cubes and add it to the pan. Cook gently 5 minutes more, stirring frequently.

3. Peel and chop the tomatoes, add them to the pan, stir well. Simmer until a sauce begins to form. Stir in the seasoning, parsley and peas.

4. Transfer the mixture to a greased casserole.

5. Heat the remaining oil and sauté the breadcrumbs until crisp. Add the sesame seeds. Sprinkle the mixture over the vegetables.

6. Bake at 350°F/180°C (Gas Mark 4) 15–20 minutes.

7. Meanwhile make the sauce. Heat the oil, cook the flour briefly then gradually pour in the water, stirring continually. As the sauce thickens add the tahini. Adjust the consistency. Pour into a jug and hand round at the table for those who wish to pour a little over the crumble.

Buckwheat Pancakes

Imperial (Metric)
For pancakes:
3 oz (85g) wholemeal flour
2 oz (55g) buckwheat flour
1 oz (30g) soya flour
pinch salt
approximately ½ pint (285ml)
water
vegetable oil for frying
For filling:
1 bunch watercress
6 oz (170g) mushrooms
approximately 3 oz (85g) vegan
margarine
1 oz (30g) wholemeal flour
⅓ pint (200ml) soya milk
seasoning to taste
pinch nutmeg
3 tomatoes
extra watercress to garnish

American
For pancakes:
¾ cup whole wheat flour
½ cup buckwheat flour
¼ cup soy flour
pinch salt
1⅓ cups water
vegetable oil for frying
For filling:
1 bunch watercress
3 cups mushrooms
⅓ cup vegan margarine
¼ cup whole wheat flour
¾ cup soy milk
seasoning to taste
pinch nutmeg
3 tomatoes
extra watercress to garnish

1. Sift together the 3 flours and salt. Stir in enough water to make a light, creamy batter. Whisk well and set aside briefly.

2. Trim and wash the watercress; slice the mushrooms. Heat 1 oz (30g or 2 tablespoons) of the margarine and sauté the watercress and mushrooms gently to soften. Remove them from the pan.

3. In a clean pan melt half the remaining margarine, add the flour then the milk, heat and stir until the sauce thickens. Add seasoning, nutmeg, and mushrooms and watercress.

4. To make the pancakes, heat a very small amount of oil in a heavy-based frying pan. Whisk the batter and adjust the consistency if necessary. Pour just enough batter into the pan to cover the base in a thin coat. Cook until brown underneath then turn carefully and cook the other side. Keep the pancakes warm while using the rest of the batter in the same way.

5. Fill each pancake with some of the mixture, roll up and arrange side by side in a shallow ovenproof dish. Decorate with slices of tomato and add the rest of the margarine in small knobs. Bake at 375°F/190°C (Gas Mark 5) 10–15 minutes. Serve garnished with watercress sprigs.

COURGETTE (ZUCCHINI) BOATS

Imperial (Metric)	American
8 even-sized courgettes	8 even-sized zucchini
2 tablespoons vegetable oil	2 tablespoons vegetable oil
1 onion, chopped	1 onion, chopped
1½ oz (45g) cashew nuts, chopped	⅓ cup cashew nuts, chopped
1 cooking apple, grated	1 cooking apple, grated
2 sticks celery, finely sliced	2 stalks celery, finely sliced
1 oz (30g) raisins	2 tablespoons raisins
seasoning to taste	seasoning to taste
1 tablespoon chopped parsley	1 tablespoon chopped parsley

1. Wash the courgettes (zucchini) and cut into halves lengthways. Blanch in a saucepan of boiling water 5 minutes only. Drain them well. When cool enough to handle use a spoon to scoop out the seeds and a little of the flesh so there is room for the filling. Arrange the boats side by side in a greased, shallow ovenproof dish.

2. Heat the oil and sauté the onion a few minutes. Add the nuts and cook until they begin to colour.

3. Stir in the apple and celery. Cook 5 minutes more or until apple and celery are tender. Add the raisins, seasoning and parsley.

4. Spoon the mixture into the courgette boats. Cover the dish with a lid or foil and bake at 375°F/190°C (Gas Mark 5) 30 minutes or until cooked.

WHOLEWHEAT AND BRUSSELS BAKE

Imperial (Metric)	American
½ lb (225g) wholewheat berries	1 cup whole wheat berries
3 tablespoons vegetable oil	3 tablespoons vegetable oil
1 lb (455g) Brussels sprouts, trimmed	1 pound Brussels sprouts, trimmed
¾ lb (340g) chestnuts, blanched and peeled	¾ pound chestnuts, blanched and peeled
1 onion, chopped	1 onion, chopped
1 clove garlic, crushed	1 clove garlic, crushed
1 stick celery, sliced	1 stalk celery, sliced
1 small red pepper, sliced	1 small red pepper, sliced
generous squeeze lemon juice	generous squeeze lemon juice
seasoning to taste	seasoning to taste
vegan margarine (optional)	vegan margarine (optional)
parsley to garnish	parsley to garnish

1. Put the wheat berries into a large pan with 1 tablespoon of oil. Heat gently a few minutes, shaking the pan frequently.

2. Cover well with water, bring to a boil then lower the heat and simmer 40 minutes or until tender.

3. Meanwhile cook the chestnuts in a pan of boiling water. When just tender, remove them at once. (The time will vary depending on their size, and how fresh they are.) Cook the Brussels sprouts about 10 minutes in another pan. Drain and set aside when they are cooked but still firm.

4. Heat the remaining oil in a clean pan. Sauté the onion and garlic a few minutes. Add the celery and pepper. Cook until beginning to soften.

5. Add the chestnuts (halved if they are very large) and the Brussels sprouts. Stir in the lemon juice and seasoning.

6. Drain any excess water from the wheat berries. Spoon them into a shallow ovenproof dish. Top with the Brussels sprouts mixture, spreading it evenly. If the ingredients seem dry, dot with some margarine.

7. Cover the dish with a lid or foil. Bake at 325°F/170°C (Gas Mark 3) about 20 minutes or until heated through. Serve at once, garnished with fresh parsley.

BAKING AND BREADS

SESAME SUNFLOWER COOKIES

Imperial (Metric)	American
2 oz (55g) raw cane sugar	⅓ cup raw cane sugar
2 oz (55g) vegan margarine	¼ cup vegan margarine
2 tablespoons (30ml) golden or maple syrup	2 tablespoons maple syrup
6 oz (170g) wholemeal flour	1½ cups whole wheat flour
1 heaped teaspoon baking powder	1 heaping teaspoon baking powder
½ oz (15g) sesame seeds	1 generous tablespoon sesame seeds
½ oz (15g) sunflower seeds	1 generous tablespoon sunflower seeds

1. In a bowl cream the sugar, margarine and syrup. Sift together the flour and baking powder and sprinkle gradually onto the sugar and margarine using fingertips to mix very thoroughly. Add the seeds.

2. On a floured board roll out the dough to about ¼ inch (6mm) thickness. Use a cutter or small glass to divide the dough into circles and arrange them on a greased baking sheet. Bake at 350°F/180°C (Gas Mark 4) 15 minutes or until a light gold in colour. Cool on the sheet then store in an airtight tin.

BANANA OAT BARS

Imperial (Metric)	American
3 oz (85g) vegan margarine	⅓ cup vegan margarine
1 tablespoon (15ml) golden or maple syrup	1 tablespoon maple syrup
1 large ripe banana, mashed	1 large ripe banana, mashed
½ lb (225g) rolled oats	2 cups rolled oats
1 oz (30g) desiccated coconut	⅓ cup desiccated coconut
1 oz (30g) cashew pieces, chopped	2 tablespoons cashew pieces, chopped
2 oz (55g) sultanas	⅓ cup golden seedless raisins

1. Melt the margarine and syrup, stirring to blend. Cool slightly. Add the banana.

2. Stir in the oats, coconut, cashew pieces and sultanas, making sure everything is well blended.

3. Turn the mixture into a shallow, lightly greased tin and press down firmly, smoothing the top. Mark into bars.

4. Bake at 350°F/180°C (Gas Mark 4) 30 minutes. Leave to cool before cutting into bars.

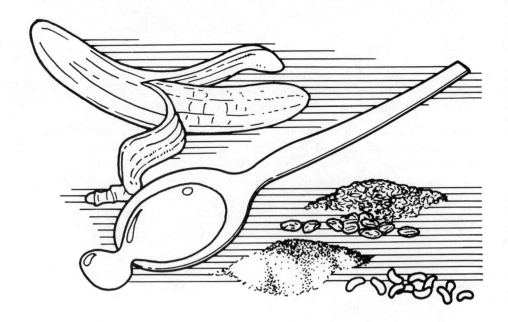

ALMOND BISCUITS

Imperial (Metric)
4 oz (115g) wholemeal semolina
4 oz (115g) soya flour
4 oz (115g) vegan margarine
4 oz (115g) raw cane sugar
water to mix
½–1 teaspoon natural almond essence
glacé cherries (washed and halved) or candied lemon slices

American
1 cup whole wheat semolina
1 cup soy flour
½ cup vegan margarine
½ cup raw cane sugar
water to mix
½–1 teaspoon natural almond extract
glacé cherries (washed and halved) or candied lemon slices

1. Sift together the semolina and flour, then use your fingers to rub in the margarine to make a crumb-like mixture.

2. Stir in the sugar. Add enough water to make a stiff dough; flavour with the almond essence. Knead briefly.

3. On a floured board roll out the dough to about ¼ inch (6mm) thickness. Cut into circles. Top with the washed, halved cherries or candied lemon slices. (You could use half of each.)

4. Arrange on a lightly greased baking sheet. Bake at 375°F/190°C (Gas Mark 5) about 20 minutes or until crisp. Cool on a wire rack.

PLAIN CHOCOLATE DIGESTIVE (GRAHAM FLOUR) BISCUITS

Imperial (Metric)	*American*
4 oz (115g) wholemeal flour	1 cup graham flour
4 oz (115g) fine oats	1 cup quick-cooking oats
pinch salt	pinch salt
4 oz (115g) vegan margarine	½ cup vegan margarine
1 oz (30g) raw cane sugar	2 tablespoons raw cane sugar
½ teaspoon bicarbonate of soda	½ teaspoon baking soda
2–3 tablespoons soya milk	2–3 tablespoons soy milk
approximately 4 oz (115g) plain chocolate	4 ounces semi-sweet chocolate

1. Mix the flour, oats and salt.

2. Rub the margarine into the flour. When the mixture has the consistency of crumbs stir in the sugar.

3. Dissolve the bicarbonate of soda by whisking it into the soya milk. Add to the dry ingredients to make a dough (you may need a drop more liquid). Knead briefly.

4. Roll out the dough to about ⅛ inch (3mm) in depth. Cut into 2½ inch (6cm) circles. Arrange on lightly greased baking sheets and prick with a fork.

5. Bake at 400°F/200°C (Gas Mark 6) 10–15 minutes or until crisp and golden. Set aside to cool.

6. Coarsely grate the chocolate and put it in a bowl over a saucepan of hot water (or a double boiler). When it has melted, either dip the biscuits into it to coat one side or spread the chocolate with a knife. Leave to set.

BRANDY SNAPS

Imperial (Metric)	American
2 oz (55g) vegan margarine	¼ cup vegan margarine
2 oz (55g) raw cane sugar	⅓ cup raw cane sugar
2 oz (55g) golden or maple syrup	¼ cup maple syrup
1 teaspoon lemon juice	1 teaspoon lemon juice
2 oz (55g) wholemeal flour	½ cup whole wheat flour
1 teaspoon ground ginger	½ teaspoon ground ginger
½ teaspoon baking powder	½ teaspoon baking powder
thick soya custard (optional)	thick soy custard (optional)

1. Melt the margarine with the sugar, syrup and lemon juice.

2. Sift together the flour, ginger and baking powder and stir into the first mixture, making sure they are well blended.

3. Drop teaspoonsful of the mixture onto well-greased baking sheets, allowing room for them to spread.

4. Bake at 375°F/190°C (Gas Mark 5) 8–10 minutes or until well spread out and beginning to get hard around the edges.

5. Leave to cool literally a minute or two then roll each biscuit around the greased handle of a wooden spoon and hold there a few seconds. Slip the roll off the spoon, and do the same with the remaining biscuits, working carefully but quickly. (If they begin to set on the tray, put them back in the oven a minute or two more).

6. Leave to cool on a wire rack. Store in an airtight tin. Brandy snaps can be served as they are or—for special occasions—filled with thick soya custard. (You can use the custard recipe in Rhubarb Fool, page 141, but made with a little less milk so it is thick enough to fill the brandy snaps.)

Hazelnut Shortbread

Imperial (Metric)
6 oz (170g) wholemeal flour
2 level teaspoons baking powder
6 oz (170g) vegan margarine
4 oz (115g) raw cane sugar
4 oz (115g) roasted hazelnuts

American
1½ cups whole wheat flour
2 level teaspoons baking powder
¾ cup vegan margarine
⅔ cup raw cane sugar
1 cup roasted hazelnuts

1. Sift the flour and baking powder.

2. Use fingertips to rub the margarine into the flour to make a fine, crumb-like mixture.

3. Stir in the sugar then the nuts, finely chopped or coarsely ground. Mix well.

4. Divide the mixture between 2 greased Swiss roll tins and press down firmly, smoothing the top as you do so.

5. Bake at 300°F/150°C (Gas Mark 2) about 30 minutes or until beginning to colour. Cut into slices while hot, but do not remove from the tin until cool. Leave on a wire rack to get completely cold.

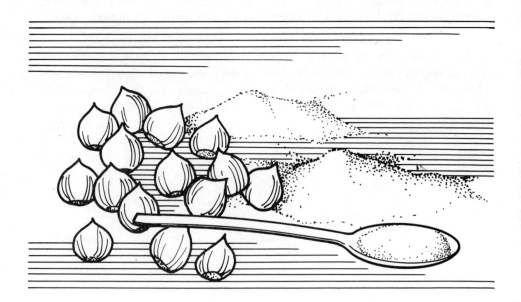

Hot Cross Buns

Imperial (Metric)
**approximately ¼ pint (140ml)
warm water
½ oz (15g) dried yeast
1 oz (30g) raw cane sugar
¾ lb (340g) wholemeal flour
pinch salt
1 teaspoon mixed spices
1 oz (30g) vegan margarine
2 oz (55g) candied peel
4 oz (115g) currants**
For glaze:
**1 oz (30g) raw cane sugar
1 tablespoon hot water**

American
**approximately ⅔ cup warm water
1 tablespoon dried yeast
2 tablespoons raw cane sugar
3 cups whole wheat flour
pinch salt
1 teaspoon mixed spices
2½ tablespoons vegan margarine
2 ounces candied fruit peel
⅔ cup currants**
For glaze:
**2 tablespoons raw cane sugar
1 tablespoon hot water**

1. Mix a drop of the warm water together with the yeast and sugar, stirring well so that they dissolve. Set aside in a warm spot 5 minutes or until frothy.

2. Sift the flour, salt and spice. Use fingertips to rub in the margarine. Make a well in the centre and pour in the yeast mixture and remaining water, kneading well to make a firm but pliable dough.

3. Add the peel and currants, distributing them as evenly as possible.

4. Put in a warm spot and leave an hour or until dough doubles in size.

5. Divide into 12 and shape into rounds. Place on a warm baking sheet and set aside again to rise.

6. Mark a cross on the top of each with the back of a knife.

7. Bake at 400°F/200°C (Gas Mark 6) about 10 minutes or until cooked.

8. Dissolve the sugar in the water and brush the hot buns with the mixture to glaze. Cool on a wire rack.

PEANUT BUTTER MUFFINS

Imperial (Metric)	American
½ lb (225g) wholemeal flour	2 cups whole wheat flour
2 level teaspoons baking powder	2 level teaspoons baking powder
2 teaspoons soya flour	2 teaspoons soy flour
pinch salt	pinch salt
1 oz (30g) vegan margarine	2½ tablespoons vegan margarine
4 oz (115g) crunchy peanut butter	¾ cup peanut butter
3 oz (85g) raw cane sugar	½ cup raw cane sugar
¼ pint (140ml) soya milk	⅔ cup soy milk
¼ pint (140ml) water	⅔ cup water
2 oz (55g) sultanas	⅓ cup golden seedless raisins

1. Sift the flour, baking powder, soya flour and salt together.

2. In another bowl beat the margarine to soften then cream with the peanut butter until well mixed. Add the sugar.

3. Tip the dry ingredients into the second bowl, stir in the milk and water then beat to lighten. The mixture should be like a batter. Add the sultanas (golden seedless raisins).

4. Oil 12 muffin tins and spoon in the batter so that each one is about ⅔ full.

5. Bake at 400°F/200°C (Gas Mark 6) 30–35 minutes or until cooked. Transfer to a wire rack when cool enough to handle. Serve warm or cold (preferably on the same day) with margarine and your favourite jam.

STRAWBERRY TARTS

Imperial (Metric)	American
For pastry:	*For pastry:*
6 oz (170g) wholemeal flour	1½ cups whole wheat flour
3 oz (85g) vegan margarine	⅓ cup vegan margarine
squeeze lemon juice	squeeze lemon juice
2–3 tablespoons cold water	2–3 tablespoons cold water
For filling:	*For filling:*
¾ lb (340g) small strawberries	12 ounces small strawberries
⅓ pint (200ml) water	¾ cup water
1 teaspoon rosewater	1 teaspoon rosewater
1 teaspoon raw cane sugar	1 teaspoon raw cane sugar
1 teaspoon arrowroot	1 teaspoon arrowroot
rose petals to garnish (optional)	rose petals to garnish (optional)

1. Put the flour in a bowl and rub in the margarine to make a crumb-like mixture.

2. Add lemon juice and enough water to make a dough. Knead briefly, then wrap in clingfilm (plastic wrap) and chill 30 minutes.

3. Roll the dough out on a floured board to ¼ inch (6mm) thickness. Cut into circles and line 8 small plain or fluted tins; press down firmly. Prick the bases.

4. Bake the tarts blind at 375°F/190°C (Gas Mark 5) 10–12 minutes until crisp and golden. Set aside.

5. Meanwhile wash and hull the strawberries.

6. Put most of the water into a small saucepan. Mix the rest of the water and the rosewater with the sugar and arrowroot then add this mixture to the saucepan. Stir well. Heat gently and continue to stir until the sauce thickens and clears.

7. Arrange the strawberries in the tarts. Pour a little of the arrowroot mixture over each, spreading it evenly. Return the tarts to the oven 2 minutes only.

8. Allow to cool. Sprinkle with a few rose petals, if liked, before serving.

NOTE: Wild strawberries are especially tasty and look attractive in small tarts of this kind. If they are not available, use small cultivated strawberries or cut larger ones in half.

COFFEE AND PRUNE SCONES

Imperial (Metric)
approximately ⅛ pint (70ml) hot coffee
2 oz (55g) stoned prunes
½ lb (225g) wholemeal flour
1 generous teaspoon baking powder
1 oz (30g) vegan margarine
1 oz (30g) raw cane sugar
1 oz (30g) chopped walnuts

American
¼ cup hot coffee
⅓ cup pitted prunes
2 cups whole wheat flour
1 generous teaspoon baking powder
2½ tablespoons vegan margarine
2 tablespoons raw cane sugar
3 tablespoons chopped walnuts

1. Pour the coffee over the prunes and leave to soak 30 minutes to an hour or until soft. Chop the flesh into small pieces.

2. Sift the flour and baking powder. Use your fingertips to rub in the margarine. Add the sugar, prunes and enough liquid to make a medium-soft dough.

3. On a floured board roll out the dough to a depth of about ¾ inch (2cm). Cut into rounds. Sprinkle with walnuts, pressing them into the dough.

4. Arrange on a greased baking sheet. Bake at 400°F/200°C (Gas Mark 6) for 15–20 minutes or until the scones are firm to the touch.

5. Transfer to a wire rack and leave to cool slightly. Best served while still warm. Delicious with homemade jam or apple butter.

Carrot Cake with Coconut Topping

Imperial (Metric)	American
¾ lb (340g) carrots	5 medium-sized carrots (about ¾ pound)
4 oz (115g) sultanas	⅔ cup golden seedless raisins
3 oz (85g) vegan margarine	⅓ cup vegan margarine
½ lb (225g) raw cane sugar	1⅓ cups raw cane sugar
½ pint (285ml) water	1⅓ cups water
10 oz (285g) wholemeal flour	2¼ cups whole wheat flour
1½ teaspoons bicarbonate of soda	1½ teaspoons baking soda
1 teaspoon mace	1 teaspoon mace
1 teaspoon cinnamon	1 teaspoon cinnamon
1 teaspoon allspice	1 teaspoon allspice
generous pinch salt	generous pinch salt
1 teaspoon natural vanilla essence	1 teaspoon natural vanilla extract
2 tablespoons grated orange peel	2 tablespoons grated orange peel
4 oz (115g) pecan or walnuts, coarsely chopped	1 cup pecan or walnuts, coarsely chopped
For topping:	*For topping:*
4 oz (115g) vegan margarine	½ cup vegan margarine
2 oz (55g) raw cane sugar, powdered in a grinder	⅓ cup raw cane sugar, powdered in a grinder
3 oz (85g) desiccated coconut	1 cup desiccated coconut

1. Peel and grate the carrots and put them into a large saucepan with the sultanas (golden seedless raisins), margarine, sugar and water.

2. Bring gently to a boil then lower the heat and simmer a few minutes. Set aside to cool slightly.

3. In a bowl mix the flour, bicarbonate of soda, spices and salt.

4. Stir the vanilla into the carrot mixture then pour onto the dry ingredients and mix very thoroughly. Add the peel and nuts.

5. Put the mixture in a greased tin and bake at 350°F/180°C (Gas Mark 4) 30–40 minutes or until a sharp knife inserted in the centre comes out clean.

6. Leave to cool then transfer carefully to a metal rack and set aside to get completely cold.

7. Meanwhile blend the margarine and sugar. When light and fluffy stir in the coconut. Smooth the topping over the carrot cake shortly before serving. Cut into squares.

Apple Raisin Cake

Imperial (Metric)	American
½ lb (225g) wholemeal flour	2 cups whole wheat flour
2 teaspoons baking powder	2 teaspoons baking powder
4 oz (115g) vegan margarine	½ cup vegan margarine
4 oz (115g) raw cane sugar	⅔ cup raw cane sugar
1 large dessert apple	1 large dessert apple
1–1½ teaspoons cinnamon	1–1½ teaspoons cinnamon
4 oz (115g) raisins	⅔ cup raisins
approximately ¼ pint (140ml) apple juice	⅔ cup apple juice

1. Sift together the flour and baking powder.

2. Rub in the margarine and, when crumbly, add the sugar.

3. Peel, core and dice the apple. Add to the first mixture together with the cinnamon and raisins. Mix well.

4. Stir in just enough apple juice to give the batter a soft dropping consistency.

5. Pour into a lightly greased 7-inch (18cm) round tin, or equivalent. Bake at 300°F/150°C (Gas Mark 2) about 1 hour or until the top is firm and a sharp knife inserted comes out clean.

6. Cool slightly then turn the cake out very carefully and leave on a wire rack to get completely cold. Best eaten within a few days.

FRANCESCA'S CAROB CAKE

Imperial (Metric)	American
6 oz (170g) wholemeal flour	1½ cups whole wheat flour
6 oz (170g) raw cane sugar	1 cup raw cane sugar
3 tablespoons carob powder	3 tablespoons carob powder
1 teaspoon bicarbonate of soda	1 teaspoon baking soda
generous pinch salt	generous pinch salt
1 teaspoon natural vanilla essence	1 teaspoon natural vanilla extract
6 tablespoons vegetable oil	6 tablespoons vegetable oil
generous ⅓ pint (200ml) water	generous ¾ cup water
For lemon curd:	*For lemon curd:*
2 oz (55g) vegan margarine	¼ cup vegan margarine
6 oz (170g) raw cane sugar	1 cup raw cane sugar
2 large lemons	2 large lemons
3 oz (85g) arrowroot	¾ cup arrowroot

1. Mix the flour, sugar, carob, bicarbonate of soda (baking soda) and salt.

2. Stir in the vanilla, oil and water, mixing them well to make a thick, moist batter.

3. Pour into a lightly greased 9-inch (23cm) square tin. Smooth the top. Bake at 350°F/180°C (Gas Mark 4) about 30-35 minutes or until a sharp knife inserted comes out clean.

4. Cool slightly, remove carefully from the tin and transfer to a wire rack to get completely cold.

5. To make the lemon curd, stir together the melted margarine and sugar, then add the juice of the lemons and the arrowroot. Heat gently until the mixture thickens. Set aside to cool.

6. Carefully slice the cake across (you can cut it into halves first, if you prefer, or even into individual squares). Spread with the lemon curd, replace the top half. Serve fairly soon after filling.

NOTE Any unused lemon curd can be stored in a jar in the fridge and used as a spread when needed.

LINZER TORTE

Imperial (Metric)	American
4 oz (115g) ground hazelnuts	1 cup ground hazelnuts
4 oz (115g) wholemeal flour	1 cup whole wheat flour
½ teaspoon ground cinnamon	½ teaspoon ground cinnamon
3 oz (85g) vegan margarine	⅓ cup vegan margarine
2 oz (55g) raw cane sugar	⅓ cup raw cane sugar
1 teaspoon grated lemon peel	1 teaspoon grated lemon peel
½ oz (15g) soya flour	2 tablespoons soy flour
⅛ pint (70ml) water	¼ cup water
½ teaspoon vegetable oil	½ teaspoon vegetable oil
½ lb (225g) raspberry jam	8 ounces raspberry jam

1. Mix together the nuts, flour and cinnamon.

2. Use fingertips to rub the margarine into the dry ingredients to make a crumb-like mixture. Stir in the sugar and grated lemon peel.

3. Mix the soya flour into the water, pour into a pan and heat gently, stirring, a few minutes. Add the oil.

4. Combine the two mixtures to make a firm dough (use a drop more water if necessary). Knead briefly. Put aside just under a quarter of the dough.

5. Grease an 8-inch (20cm) flan ring and a baking sheet. Press the larger piece of dough evenly around the bottom and sides of the ring.

6. Spread the jam over the base of the flan.

7. Roll out the remaining dough, cut into strips and use them to make a latticework pattern over the jam. If necessary, trim or turn down the sides of the flan so they do not stand too high above the filling.

8. Bake at 375°F/190°C (Gas Mark 5) 35–45 minutes or until golden and crisp. Cool slightly before carefully removing the ring. Serve warm or cold.

PARKIN

Imperial (Metric)	American
½ lb (225g) wholemeal flour	2 cups whole wheat flour
1 teaspoon bicarbonate of soda	1 teaspoon baking soda
4 oz (115g) rolled oats	1 cup rolled oats
1 teaspoon mixed spice	1 teaspoon pumpkin pie spice
1 teaspoon ground ginger	1 teaspoon ground ginger
4 oz (115g) molasses	¼ cup molasses
4 oz (115g) raw cane sugar	⅔ cup raw cane sugar
4 oz (115g) vegan margarine	½ cup vegan margarine
1 oz (30g) almonds, chopped (optional)	¼ cup almonds, chopped (optional)

1. Sift the flour and bicarbonate of soda; stir in the oats and spices.

2. Put the molasses, sugar and margarine in a saucepan and heat gently, stirring with a wooden spoon until well blended.

3. Pour the warm mixture into the dry ingredients and beat a few minutes to mix.

4. Grease a medium-sized square tin thoroughly. Sprinkle with the chopped nuts, if using them. Pour in the mixture.

5. Bake at 325°F/170°C (Gas Mark 3) 1–1¼ hours or until firm to touch and a fine knife inserted comes out clean. Cool slightly, then carefully turn out on a wire rack and leave to become cold. If stored in an airtight tin a day or two the flavour will improve.

NOTE: Although the cake can be baked in a tin that has simply been well greased, it will be easier to remove if you line it with greased greaseproof (waxed) paper, then proceed as above.

TAHINI CAKE

Imperial (Metric)	American
¾ lb (340g) wholemeal flour	3 cups whole wheat flour
3 teaspoons baking powder	3 teaspoons baking powder
1 teaspoon bicarbonate of soda	1 teaspoon baking soda
6 oz (170g) raw cane sugar	1 cup raw cane sugar
2 oz (55g) walnuts, chopped	½ cup walnuts, chopped
2 oz (55g) raisins	⅓ cup raisins
2 oz (55g) candied peel	2 ounces candied fruit peel
4 oz (115g) tahini	scant ½ cup tahini
⅓ pint (200ml) orange juice	¾ cup orange juice
⅓ pint (200ml) water	¾ cup water

1. Sift the flour, baking powder and soda.

2. Stir in the sugar, nuts, raisins and peel.

3. Whisk together the tahini, orange juice and water. When well blended add to the dry ingredients. The mixture should be thick and smooth—if too dry add more orange juice.

4. Pour into a large square tin, first lining it with greased greaseproof (waxed) paper. Smooth the top.

5. Bake at 350°F/180°C (Gas Mark 4) 45 minutes to 1 hour. Test the cake with a sharp knife—when it comes out dry remove the cake from the oven and leave to cool slightly.

6. Transfer to a wire rack. Cut into squares when completely cold.

TWO-GRAIN BREAD

Imperial (Metric)	American
1/8 pint (70ml) warm water	1/4 cup warm water
1/2 oz (15g) dried yeast	1 tablespoon dried yeast
2 oz (55g) raw cane sugar	1/3 cup raw cane sugar
1 1/2 oz (45g) vegan margarine	3 1/2 tablespoons vegan margarine
pinch salt	pinch salt
1/2 lb (225g) rolled oats	2 cups rolled oats
1/3 pint (200ml) boiling water	3/4 cup boiling water
1/3 pint (200ml) cold water	3/4 cup cold water
approximately 1 lb (455g) wholemeal flour	approximately 4 cups whole wheat flour

1. Put the warm water into a small bowl and whisk in the yeast plus a teaspoon of the sugar. When dissolved set aside in a warm spot and leave until frothy.

2. When ready, use another bowl to mix together the remaining sugar, margarine, salt and oats. Add the boiling water to melt the margarine.

3. Pour in the yeast mixture and the cold water. Mix thoroughly. Gradually add enough flour to make a firm but elastic dough. Knead until smooth.

4. Put the dough in a lightly greased bowl, cover and leave in a warm spot to double in size.

5. Knock back (punch down) the dough, knead briefly. Divide into two even-sized pieces and shape them into loaves. Place in 2 lightly greased loaf tins and set aside to double in size again.

7. Bake the bread at 350°F/180°C (Gas Mark 4) 50 minutes or until they sound hollow when tapped with the knuckles. Put on a wire rack to cool.

INDIAN BREADS

CHAPATTIS

Imperial (Metric)	American
½ lb (225g) wholemeal flour	2 cups whole wheat flour
generous pinch salt	generous pinch salt
cold water to mix	cold water to mix
1 oz (30g) roasted sesame seeds	generous tablespoon roasted sesame seeds

1. Sift together the flour and salt. Add just enough cold water to make a firm but pliable dough and knead well.

2. Add the sesame seeds and continue kneading so that they are evenly distributed and the dough is smooth.

3. Break the dough into small balls (there should be enough for about 8–12, depending on size). Roll out on a floured board to make into very thin circles.

4. Heat a heavy-based frying pan until hot and cook the chapattis, 1 or 2 at a time, literally ½ minute. When dough begins to "blister", turn at once and cook the other side.

5. Wrap cooked chapattis lightly in a tea or dish towel and keep them warm while using the rest of the dough in the same way.

GRAM CHAPATTIS

Imperial (Metric)	American
4 oz (115g) wholemeal flour	1 cup whole wheat flour
4 oz (115g) gram (chickpea) flour	¾ cup gram (chickpea) flour
cold water to mix	cold water to mix

1. Sift the flours then follow instructions as for ordinary chapattis. Gram chapattis are slightly higher in protein and are a little heavier in texture.

PURIS

Imperial (Metric)	American
12 oz (340g) wholemeal flour	3 cups whole wheat flour
pinch salt	pinch salt
2 oz (55g) vegan margarine	¼ cup vegan margarine
cold water to mix	cold water to mix
vegetable oil for frying	vegetable oil for frying

1. Sift together the flour and salt. Rub most of the margarine into the dry ingredients to make a crumb-like mixture.

2. Add enough cold water to make a fairly firm dough, knead briefly then set aside ½ hour.

3. Knead briefly again then divide the dough into 8–12 balls. Press them out into rounds.

4. Melt the remaining margarine and brush both sides of the puris lightly with it.

5. Heat vegetable oil in a pan. When hot, deep fry the puris a few at a time. They should colour in 10–20 seconds, then scoop them out with a slotted spoon, drain on paper towels and keep them warm while cooking the remaining rounds in the same way.

NOTE: Although these breads can be made quite well with wholemeal flour, they are also tasty when made the traditional way, with white flour.

PITA BREAD

Imperial (Metric)
½ lb (225g) wholemeal flour
pinch salt
¼ pint (140ml) warm water
¼ oz (7g) fresh yeast
½ teaspoonful raw cane sugar

American
2 cups whole wheat flour
pinch salt
⅔ cup warm water
2 teaspoons fresh yeast
½ teaspoon raw cane sugar

1. Sift the flour and salt.

2. In a small bowl whisk together the water, yeast and sugar. When the yeast has dissolved set the bowl aside in a warm spot 10–20 minutes or until frothy.

3. Pour the liquid onto the dry ingredients and stir to make a dough. Knead the dough until smooth. Put into a greased bowl, cover and leave in a warm spot until doubled in size.

4. Knead the dough lightly. Break into 4 even-sized pieces and roll each one into an oval shape. Arrange on a greased baking sheet and bake at 400°F/200°C (Gas Mark 6) about 10 minutes or until well risen.

5. Cool slightly on a wire rack. Pita bread can be served warm or cold and is usually halved and then slit open to make a pocket which can be filled with salad, vegetables, falafels or whatever you like.

ONION BAGELS

Imperial (Metric)
12 oz (340g) wholemeal flour
pinch salt
½ oz (15g) fresh yeast
generous ⅓ pint (200ml) warm water
2 teaspoons vegetable oil
approximately 1 oz (30g) vegan margarine
½ small onion, finely chopped

American
3 cups whole wheat flour
pinch salt
1 generous tablespoon fresh yeast
generous ¾ cup warm water
2 teaspoons vegetable oil
2½ tablespoons vegan margarine
½ small onion, finely chopped

1. Sift the flour and salt into a bowl.

2. Mix the yeast in about half the water. When dissolved add 4 oz (115g or 1 cup) of the flour. Put into a bowl, cover and set aside in a warm spot. Leave 30 minutes or until doubled in size.

3. Add the rest of the water, the flour and finally the oil. Knead the dough well until smooth.

4. Return the dough to the bowl, cover and leave in a warm spot to double in size. Knock it back (punch it down), and then leave again for about 15 minutes.

5. Knead the dough briefly once more before breaking it into small rounds (this amount of ingredients should make approximately 8). Shape into thin strands about 6 inches (15cm) long, forming these into circles and pushing the ends together.

6. Arrange on a floured board, cover and leave in warm spot 20–30 minutes.

7. Heat the oven to 400°F/200°C (Gas Mark 6) so that it is ready for the bagels.

8. Bring a large pan of water to a boil and then lower to simmering. Gently drop in the pieces of dough, a few at a time. Use a slotted spoon to scoop them out the moment they rise to the surface, place them at once on a greased baking sheet and put them straight into the oven.

9. Bake 20 minutes or until golden brown. If liked, you can turn them over so that they colour more evenly.

10. Meanwhile heat most of the margarine and sauté the onion until crisp and brown.

11. Brush the bagels with margarine, top with onion, brush lightly with more margarine. Leave to cool.

DESSERTS AND OTHER SWEET TREATS

MAPLE PECAN ICE-CREAM

Imperial (Metric)	American
¾ teaspoon agar agar	¾ teaspoon agar agar
3 tablespoons maple syrup syrup	3 tablespoons maple syrup
1 pint (570ml) soya milk	2½ cups soy milk
1 teaspoon natural vanilla essence	1 teaspoon natural vanilla extract
2 oz (55g) pecan nuts, coarsely broken	½ cup pecan nuts, coarsely broken
maple syrup to serve (optional)	maple syrup to serve (optional)

1. Whisk together the agar agar, maple syrup and soya milk. Pour into a small saucepan and bring gently to just below boiling point, stirring continually.

2. Remove the pan from the heat and add the vanilla and pecan nuts, blending them thoroughly.

3. Pour the mixture into a freezing tray (ice tray) and allow to cool. Turn freezer to the lowest setting and stand the tray inside 1 hour.

4. Turn the mixture into a bowl and beat well, then return it to the tray. Refreeze until firm. Remove the ice-cream from the freezer a short while before serving. Delicious with a little extra maple syrup served on top.

Tofu Lemon Flan

Imperial (Metric)

For flan:
½ lb (225g) vegan digestive
biscuits
4 oz (115g) vegan margarine,
melted

For filling:
6 tablespoons golden or maple
syrup
1 oz (30g) conflour
¾ pint (425ml) water
½ lb (225g) tofu
6 tablespoons lemon juice
1 tablespoon grated lemon rind
green and black grapes

American

For flan:
8 ounces vegan graham crackers
½ cup vegan margarine, melted

For filling:
6 tablespoons maple syrup
¼ cup cornflour
2 cups water
1 cup tofu
6 tablespoons lemon juice
1 tablespoon grated lemon rind
green and black grapes

1. Crumble the biscuits and mix with the margarine. Use the mixture to line a medium-sized flan ring placed on a baking sheet. Set aside.

2. Put the syrup, cornflour and water into a saucepan. Heat gently, stirring until the sauce thickens.

3. Mash the tofu well and combine it with the lemon juice and rind (this can be done in a blender). Add this mixture to the saucepan, stir and cook gently a few minutes more, then set aside to cool slightly.

4. Pour this mixture into the prepared flan case, top with the decoratively arranged grapes. Chill until it sets firm.

Mincemeat Vol-au-Vents

Imperial (Metric)	*American*
Puff pastry (see page 38)	**Puff pastry (see page 38)**
undiluted soya milk to serve	**Undiluted soy milk to serve**
For mincemeat:	*For mincemeat:*
1½ lbs (680g) mixed dried fruit	**4½ cups mixed dried fruit**
juice and finely grated rind of 1	**juice and finely grated rind of 1**
large lemon	**large lemon**
2 apples, grated	**2 apples, grated**
6 oz (170g) raw cane sugar	**1 cup raw cane sugar**
6 oz (170g) almonds, chopped	**1½ cups almonds, chopped**
1 teaspoon mixed spice	**1 teaspoon pumpkin pie spice**
½ teaspoon ground cinnamon	**½ teaspoon ground cinnamon**
½ teaspoon ground nutmeg	**½ teaspoon ground nutmeg**
⅛ pint (70ml) apple juice	**¼ cup apple juice**
⅓ pint (200ml) vegetable oil	**¾ cup vegetable oil**

1. Make up the mincemeat by mixing all the ingredients thoroughly, making sure they are well blended. Put into dry, sealed jars and keep in a cool spot until needed.

2. The vol-au-vents should be made up according to instructions on page 38. When cooked, fill each one with mincemeat. (If you intend to serve the vol-au-vents cold, do not fill until you are ready for them.) Top with undiluted soya milk.

NOTE: This mincemeat can also be used in more traditional ways, such as in tarts and pies. It should be refrigerated and used within a week or so. Adding a drop of alcohol (sherry, brandy or whisky) will increase the time it can be kept.

Apricot Mousse

Imperial (Metric)	American
½ lb (225g) dried apricots	1½ cups dried apricots
generous squeeze lemon juice	generous squeeze lemon juice
½ pint (285ml) orange juice	1⅓ cups orange juice
1½ teaspoons agar agar	1½ teaspoons agar agar
approximately 2 tablespoons undiluted soya milk	approximately 2 tablespoons undiluted soy milk
maple syrup and chopped pecan nuts to top	maple syrup and chopped pecan nuts to top

1. Wash the apricots then cover them with boiling water and leave to soak overnight.

2. Add lemon juice and cook the apricots gently 10–20 minutes or until tender. Set aside to cool, drain well, then mash or purée.

3. Put the orange juice in a saucepan and bring gently to a boil. Whisk in the agar agar and continue heating and whisking a few minutes.

4. Combine the apricot purée with the orange juice, stirring well. Stir in enough soya milk to give the mixture a creamy colour.

5. Divide among 4 attractive glasses and leave to cool then chill well before serving. Top with a swirl of maple syrup and some chopped nuts.

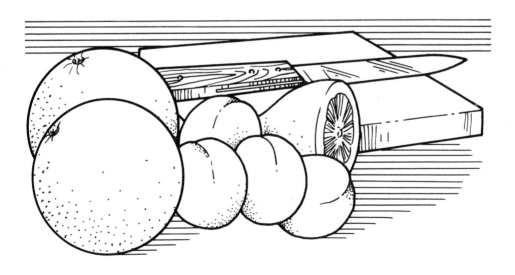

YOGURT DESSERT

Imperial (Metric)	American
1 pint (570ml) soya milk	2½ cups soy milk
yogurt starter	yogurt starter
1 oz (30g) pistachio nuts	3 tablespoons pistachio nuts
2 oz (55g) sultanas	⅓ cup golden seedless raisins
1-2 tablespoons golden or maple syrup	1-2 tablespoons maple syrup
½ teaspoon vanilla essence	½ teaspoon vanilla extract
1 tablespoon orange flower water	1 tablespoon orange flower water
2 teaspoons grated lemon peel	2 teaspoons grated lemon peel

1. In a saucepan bring the milk to a boil, stirring to prevent a skin forming. Then leave it to cool to blood heat.

2. Add the starter and stir well. Pour the mixture into a yogurt maker (you can also use a wide-necked jar, or jars, or a thermos).

3. If using an electric yogurt maker, simply switch it on. Jars will need to be placed in a warm spot. The yogurt should be set in 6–8 hours, depending on the method you are using.

4. Lightly grill the pistachios then chop them coarsely.

5. Mix together the yogurt, most of the pistachios, sultanas (golden seedless raisins), syrup, vanilla essence, the orange flower water and peel. Cover the mixture and chill well.

6. Divide the yogurt among 4 glasses and top with remaining nuts just before serving.

NOTE: Although most yogurt starters are the dairy variety, yeast cultures are now becoming available, so it is possible to make a completely vegan version. If you cannot find it in the shops, you should be able to buy ready-made soya yogurt, which can be used in the same way as described above.

RHUBARB FOOL

Imperial (Metric)	American
½ pint (285ml) soya milk	1⅓ cups soy milk
1 oz (30g) custard powder	½ tablespoon custard powder
1 oz (30g) raw cane sugar	2 tablespoons raw cane sugar
1 lb (455g) rhubarb	1 pound rhubarb
4–5 tablespoons golden or maple syrup	4–5 tablespoons maple syrup
½ teaspoon cinnamon	½ teaspoon cinnamon
extra cinnamon	extra cinnamon
plain grated chocolate or flaked almonds	grated chocolate or slivered almonds
	semi-sweetened grated chocolate or slivered almonds

1. Put most of the milk into a saucepan and bring gently to a boil.

2. Mix together the custard powder and remaining milk. Pour the hot milk onto the mixture and stir briskly; add the sugar. When the custard begins to thicken, set aside to cool.

3. Wash and trim the rhubarb then cut it into short lengths and place in a clean saucepan with the syrup and cinnamon.

4. Simmer the rhubarb gently until cooked. Push through a sieve to make a thick purée (or use a blender). Set this aside also to cool.

5. Stir together the custard and rhubarb, mixing well. Spoon into small dishes or glasses; chill briefly. Sprinkle with more cinnamon and some grated chocolate or almonds before serving. Nice with crisp biscuits such as Sesame Sunflower Cookies (page 115).

GOOSEBERRY AND ELDERFLOWER CRUMBLE

Imperial (Metric)	American
1½ lbs (680g) gooseberries	1½ pounds gooseberries
3 heads of elderflower	3 heads of elderflower
approximately 4 oz (115g) raw cane sugar	⅔ cup raw cane sugar
½ pint (285ml) water	1⅓ cups water
For crumble:	For crumble:
3 oz (85g) oatmeal	¾ cup oatmeal
approximately 2 tablespoons vegetable oil	approximately 2 tablespoons vegetable oil
2 oz (55g) sunflower seeds	½ cup sunflower seeds
1 oz (30g) desiccated coconut	⅓ cup desiccated coconut

1. Wash, top and tail the gooseberries. Put them in a saucepan.

2. Tie the elderflower heads in a piece of muslin or cheesecloth and add to the pan with the sugar and water. (Extra hard or unripe gooseberries may need more sugar.)

3. Stir the mixture then cover the pan. Cook gently 15–20 minutes or until the gooseberries are just tender. Add a spoonful or two of water if necessary, though the fruit will probably release enough juice of its own.

4. Remove the elderflowers. Spoon the gooseberries into an ovenproof dish.

5. Mix the oatmeal with enough oil to make a crumble-type mixture; add the seeds and coconut. Sprinkle the crumble evenly over the fruit then press down lightly.

6. Bake at 325°F/170°C (Gas Mark 3) 20–30 minutes or until the crumble is crisp.

NOTE: This recipe can, of course, be made without the elderflowers. But do use them when they are in season—they add a subtle but very special flavour.

BANANAS IN CIDER

Imperial (Metric)	American
½ pint (285ml) cider	1⅓ cups cider
2 tablespoons lemon juice	2 tablespoons lemon juice
1 oz (30g) raw cane sugar	2 tablespoons raw cane sugar
4 bananas	4 bananas
granola to serve	granola to serve

1. Put the cider in a frying pan with the lemon juice and sugar. Bring gently to a boil, stirring continually so that the sugar dissolves. Then lower the heat and simmer the sauce 5 minutes.

2. Peel the bananas and slice them lengthways. Put them into the pan and spoon some of the sauce over them.

3. Cover the pan and simmer the bananas 5–10 minutes, turning them occasionally. When they are tender set them aside to cool.

4. Divide among 4 dishes, spooning any extra sauce over the fruit. Chill briefly. Serve sprinkled generously with granola.

PINEAPPLE SORBET

Imperial (Metric)	American
½ lb (225g) tin pineapple pieces in natural juice	small can pineapple pieces in natural juice
⅓ pint (200ml) undiluted soya milk	¾ cup undiluted soy milk
1 tablespoon golden or maple syrup	1 tablespoon maple syrup
generous squeeze lemon juice	generous squeeze lemon juice
1 tablespoon grated lemon peel	1 tablespoon grated lemon peel
glacé cherries to garnish	glacé cherries to garnish
Cointreau (optional)	Cointreau (optional)

1. Coarsely mash or chop the pineapple pieces.

2. Add the undiluted soya milk, syrup, lemon juice and peel. Mix well.

3. Turn the mixture into a freezing tray (ice tray) and freeze until firm. Remove from the tray, break up the ice and beat to make a thick, lump-free mush.

4. Return this to the tray. Freeze again until firm.

5. Serve in tall glasses decorating each portion with a glacé cherry. A spoonful of Cointreau can be poured over the top, if liked.

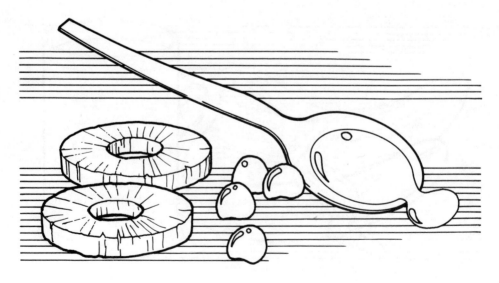

Pumpkin Pie

Imperial (Metric)	American
For flan:	*For piecrust:*
6 oz (170g) wholemeal flour	1½ cups whole wheat flour
2–3 tablespoons vegetable oil	2–3 tablespoons vegetable oil
cold water to mix	cold water to mix
1 oz (30g) roasted sesame seeds	¼ cup roasted sesame seeds
For filling:	*For filling:*
1½ lb (680g) pumpkin	1½ pounds pumpkin
2 tablespoons vegetable oil	2 tablespoons vegetable oil
1 teaspoon cinnamon	1 teaspoon cinnamon
½ teaspoon ground ginger	½ teaspoon ground ginger
¼ teaspoon ground cloves	¼ teaspoon ground cloves
4 oz (115g) raw cane sugar	⅔ cup raw cane sugar
2 tablespoons tahini	2 tablespoons tahini
2 oz (55g) walnuts	½ cup walnuts
2 oz (55g) raisins	⅓ cup raisins

1. Put the flour in a bowl, sprinkle in the oil then add just enough cold water to bind the flour to a soft dough. Add the seeds. Knead lightly then roll it out and line a medium-sized flan ring placed on a greased baking sheet (or line a well-greased pie plate).

2. Prick the base with a fork. Bake at 350°F/180°C (Gas Mark 4) 10 minutes.

3. Meanwhile, peel and chop the pumpkin. Heat the oil and sauté the pumpkin a few minutes, stirring frequently. Then cover the pan and cook the pumpkin over gentle heat until soft.

4. Drain off any excess liquid, and mash or blend the pumpkin to make a purée. Drain again if necessary.

5. Put it in a bowl. Stir in the spices, sugar, tahini, nuts and raisins, making sure all the ingredients are well mixed.

6. Spoon the mixture into the flan case (or pie plate) and bake at the same temperature 30 minutes more or until cooked. Serve hot.

NOTE: This will not have the same firm texture as pumpkin pie made with eggs. If this bothers you, try adding a few tablespoons of cooked semolina to the pumpkin mixture before baking.

CAROB SLICE WITH PINEAPPLE SAUCE

Imperial (Metric)

5 oz (140g) vegan margarine
1 oz (30g) raw cane sugar,
powdered in grinder
1 tablespoon golden or maple
syrup
2 oz (55g) carob powder
1 oz (30g) ground almonds
½ lb (225g) vegan digestive
biscuits
For sauce:
½ lb (225g) tin pineapple pieces
in natural juice, drained
½ lb (225g) tofu, drained
golden or maple syrup to sweeten
(optional)

American

generous ½ cup vegan margarine
2 tablespoons raw cane sugar,
powdered in grinder
1 tablespoon maple syrup
½ cup carob powder
¼ cup ground almonds
8 ounces vegan graham crackers
For sauce:
small can pineapple pieces in
in natural juice, drained
1 cup tofu, drained
maple syrup to sweeten (optional)

1. In a saucepan gently melt the margarine. Add the sugar, syrup and carob powder, mixing well. Add the ground nuts.

2. Crush the biscuits (graham crackers) to make them into fine crumbs. Stir them into the saucepan.

3. Turn the mixture into a lightly greased shallow tin. Press down firmly and evenly, smoothing the top. Set aside to firm up.

4. To make the sauce blend the pineapple pieces with the tofu (and syrup). Adjust the consistency, if necessary, with the reserved pineapple juice.

5. Serve the cake cut into slices and topped with the sauce.

STUFFED APPLES

Imperial (Metric)	American
4 large cooking apples	4 large cooking apples
1 oz (30g) raw cane sugar	2 tablespoons raw cane sugar
2 oz (55g) cooked brown rice	⅓ cup cooked brown rice
2 oz (55g) raisins	⅓ cup raisins
1 oz (30g) pine nuts	3 tablespoons pine nuts
1 oz (30g) vegan margarine, melted	2½ tablespoons vegan margarine, melted
ground cinnamon	ground cinnamon

1. Cut the top off each apple then carefully remove the core and some of the flesh to leave a ½-inch (1.25cm) shell.

2. Arrange the apples close together in a small ovenproof dish.

3. Mix the sugar into the rice, add the raisins and pine nuts. Stir in the melted margarine so that all the ingredients are well blended.

4. Use the rice mixture to fill the apples. Top with a sprinkling of cinnamon then replace the tops.

5. Pour hot water into the dish so that it comes half way up the sides of the apples.

6. Bake at 350°F/180°C (Gas Mark 4) 30–40 minutes or until the apples are tender. Serve hot.

CREAM OF RICE

Imperial (Metric)	American
1 oz (30g) vegan margarine	2½ tablespoons vegan margarine
1 oz (30g) pistachio nuts, chopped	3 tablespoons pistachio nuts, chopped
1 oz (30g) raisins	2 tablespoons raisins
4 oz (115g) brown rice	½ cup brown rice
¾ pint (425ml) soya milk	2 cups soy milk
4 oz (115g) raw cane sugar	⅔ cup raw cane sugar
1 teaspoon rosewater	1 teaspoon rosewater
pinch nutmeg	pinch nutmeg

1. Melt the margarine and gently sauté the nuts and raisins a few minutes. Remove from pan, drain and leave to cool.

2. In a heavy-based pan toast the dry rice over medium heat 5–10 minutes or until golden. Cool then grind to a powder.

3. Bring the milk to a boil, reduce the heat and gradually add all the rice. Simmer and stir until the mixture begins to thicken; add the sugar and continue simmering and stirring a further 10–15 minutes.

4. Flavour with the rosewater and nutmeg, cook a few minutes more then let cool slightly before pouring into individual glasses or bowls. Sprinkle with nuts and raisins. Chill.

NOTE: Although pistachio nuts make this dish more special, cashews can be used instead for a less expensive version.

MAPLE PANCAKES

Imperial (Metric)
4 oz (115g) wholemeal flour
2 oz (55g) soya flour
approximately ½ pint (285ml)
water
2 teaspoons vegetable oil
vegetable oil for frying
For sauce:
⅓ pint (200ml) maple syrup
generous squeeze lemon juice
1 oz (30g) chopped roasted
hazelnuts
lemon wedges to serve

American
1 cup whole wheat flour
½ cup soy flour
1⅓ cups water
2 teaspoons vegetable oil
vegetable oil for frying
For sauce:
¾ cup maple syrup
generous squeeze lemon juice
¼ cup chopped roasted hazelnuts
lemon wedges to serve

1. In a bowl sift the flours. Gradually add the water, whisking continually to make sure there are no lumps. Add the oil. Continue whisking to lighten the batter then set aside in the cool at least 30 minutes.

2. To make the sauce combine the maple syrup and lemon juice and cook gently 5 minutes. Add the nuts, stir and cook a few minutes more.

3. While the sauce is cooking make the pancakes. The batter should be whisked again before use and, if necessary, more water added to give it a pouring consistency.

4. Heat a drop of oil in a frying pan and when it begins to smoke pour in a thin layer of batter. Cook gently, shaking the pan occasionally, until cooked underneath. Toss the pancake and cook the other side.

5. Keep pancakes warm while using the rest of the batter in the same way.

6. Serve folded in quarters and topped with the sauce. Lemon wedges should accompany the pancakes for those who want them.

Melon Fruit Salad with Nut Cream

Imperial (Metric)	American
2 small ogen or cantaloupe melons	2 small ogens or cantaloupes
generous squeeze lemon juice	generous squeeze lemon juice
4 oz (115g) cherries	$\frac{1}{2}$ cup cherries
4 oz (115g) white grapes	$\frac{3}{4}$ cup white grapes
1 large peach, chopped	1 large peach, chopped
4 oz (115g) fresh dates	$\frac{2}{3}$ cup fresh dates
orange juice or Kirsch	orange juice or Kirsch
For nut cream:	*For nut cream:*
3 oz (85g) ground almonds	$\frac{3}{4}$ cup ground almonds
approximately $\frac{1}{4}$ teaspoon almond essence	approximately $\frac{1}{4}$ teaspoon almond extract
approximately 1 tablespoon undiluted soya milk	approximately 1 tablespoon undiluted soy milk

1. Halve the melons and scoop out the seeds. Brush the cut surfaces with lemon juice.

2. Stir together the cherries, grapes, peach and dates. Add orange juice or Kirsch to moisten.

3. Spoon the fruit into the melon halves. Chill well.

4. Meanwhile, make the nut cream by mixing the almonds and essence (extract) with the undiluted soya milk. Adjust the flavour and consistency to taste.

5. Serve the melon halves topped, if liked, with a little more Kirsch. Hand round the nut cream at the table for those who want it.

KADAIFI

Imperial (Metric)	American
½ lb (225g) walnuts	1⅔ cups walnuts
2 oz (55g) wholemeal breadcrumbs	1⅔ cups whole wheat breadcrumbs
2 oz (55g) raw cane sugar	⅓ cup raw cane sugar
¼ pint (140ml) orange juice	⅔ cup orange juice
1 lb (455g) kadaifi pastry (see note)	1 pound kadaifi pastry (see note)
½ lb (225g) vegan margarine, melted	1 cup vegan margarine, melted
For syrup:	*For syrup:*
½ lb (225g) raw cane sugar	1⅓ cups raw cane sugar
⅓ pint (200ml) water	¾ cup water
1 tablespoon lemon juice	1 tablespoon lemon juice
½–1 teaspoon cinnamon	½–1 teaspoon cinnamon

1. Chop the walnuts and stir into the breadcrumbs, sugar and orange juice.

2. Shred the pastry and stir into the margarine so that it is well coated.

3. Line a shallow, lightly greased tin with half the pastry. Top with the nut mixture, spreading it evenly. Finish with the remaining pastry. Press down evenly.

4. Bake at 350°F/180°C (Gas Mark 4) 40 minutes. Do not remove from the tin.

5. Meanwhile make a syrup by combining the listed ingredients in a small saucepan and bring them to a boil, stirring continually. When the sugar has dissolved lower the heat and continue simmering 10 minutes.

6. Pour the syrup over the hot pastry, spreading it as evenly as possible. Cover the baking tin with napkins or a clean tea or dish towel. Set aside a few hours, preferably overnight, to give the syrup time to sink in. Serve cut in squares.

NOTE: Traditionally kadaifi is soaked in double this amount of syrup, the end result being a very sweet and sticky pastry. If you want it to taste as it would in Greece or Cyprus increase the syrup accordingly. Kadaifi pastry is available in specialty shops. Made from flour and water it looks rather like Shredded Wheat. In fact you can use Shredded Wheat for this recipe, simply soaking it first in water then squeezing out the excess. It will not be the same as real kadaifi pastry, but will certainly be eaten up just as quickly.

POACHED PEARS

Imperial (Metric)	American
2 oz (55g) raw cane sugar	⅓ cup raw cane sugar
1 oz (30g) vegan margarine	2½ tablespoons vegan margarine
4 large Conference pears	4 large Bosc pears
2 tablespoons lemon juice	2 tablespoons lemon juice
ground ginger	ground ginger
1 oz (30g) flaked almonds	¼ cup slivered almonds

1. Put the sugar in a frying pan with the margarine and heat gently, stirring, until the sugar dissolves.

2. Peel the pears and remove the cores. Cut them into thick slices.

3. Add them to the frying pan and cook a few minutes then turn and cook the other side.

4. Pour in the juice and add a pinch of ground ginger. Cook gently a few minutes more until the pears are soft.

5. Serve at once, spooning any remaining sauce over the pears. Sprinkle with more ginger and some flaked almonds.

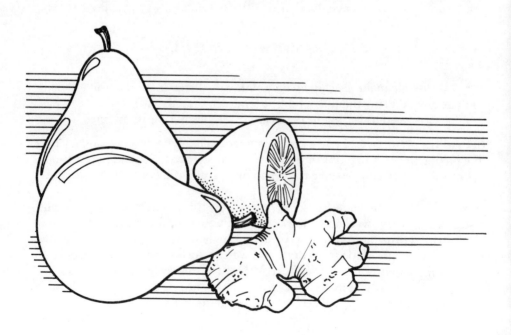

Fruit Kebabs

Imperial (Metric)	American
4 oz (115g) strawberries	¾ cup strawberries
4 oz (115g) black grapes	¾ cup black grapes
2 apples	2 apples
2 firm pears	2 firm pears
1 small melon	1 small melon
lemon juice	lemon juice
For dip:	*For dip:*
4 oz (115g) cashew nuts	1 cup cashew nuts
½ oz (15g) raw cane sugar, powdered in grinder	1 tablespoon raw cane sugar, powdered in grinder
water or undiluted soya milk to mix	water or undiluted soy milk to mix
few drops vanilla essence	few drops vanilla extract

1. Wash the strawberries and grapes; cut the unpeeled apples and pears into thick slices; cube the melon. Dip any cut fruits in lemon juice to keep their colour.

2. Use small skewers or toothpicks to spear a small selection of fruits, choosing them so that they look attractive together. Arrange these kebabs on a serving plate.

3. Make the dip by grinding the nuts to a powder then mixing them with the sugar. Stir in enough liquid to give a dip consistency; add vanilla.

4. Pass the dip around for everyone to take a few spoonsful. Hand round the kebabs.

NOTE: This is a fun dessert idea that children would probably enjoy. Make sure they are careful with the cocktail sticks.

CANDIED CHESTNUTS

Imperial (Metric)	American
14 oz (395g) chestnuts	14 ounces chestnuts
½ lb (225g) raw cane sugar	1⅓ cups raw cane sugar
8 tablespoons water	8 tablespoons water
few drops vanilla essence	few drops vanilla extract
approximately 1 oz (30g) raw cane sugar, powdered in grinder	2 tablespoons raw cane sugar, powdered in grinder

1. Peel the chestnuts and carefully remove the inner skins.

2. Put the sugar in a heavy-based saucepan. Add the water. Bring slowly to a boil, stirring continually so that the sugar dissolves completely.

3. Add the chestnuts to the syrup, stir, bring back to a boil. Add the vanilla.

4. Lower the heat and simmer until the chestnuts are tender. Remove them from any remaining liquid and drain well on paper towels.

5. Roll the chestnuts in the powdered sugar then place on greaseproof paper and leave to dry. Candied chestnuts can be served as a sweet or with coffee at the end of the meal. As a quick but special dessert, put 4 or 5 in a glass and top with vegan yogurt or nut cream.

CHOCOLATE NUT CLUSTERS

Imperial (Metric)	American
½ lb (225g) plain chocolate	8 ounces semi-sweet chocolate
1 tablespoon vegetable oil	1 tablespoon vegetable oil
3 oz (85g) roasted hazelnuts, coarsely chopped	⅔ cup roasted hazelnuts, coarsely chopped
3 oz (85g) crystallized ginger	3 ounces crystallized ginger

1. Break up the chocolate and place in a bowl suspended over a saucepan of hot water (or a double boiler).

2. Stir the chocolate gently until it melts then add the oil.

3. Off the heat quickly add the nuts and ginger mixing well so that they are evenly distributed.

4. Use a spoon to drop mounds of the mixture into small paper cases or onto a lightly greased baking sheet. Set aside until they firm up.

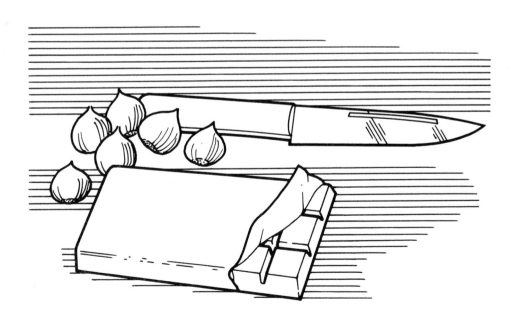

WALNUT TOFU BALLS

Imperial (Metric)	American
2 oz (55g) wholemeal cake or breadcrumbs	1 cup whole wheat cake or breadcrumbs
2 oz (55g) tofu	¼ cup tofu
generous pinch mixed spice	generous pinch mixed spices
3–4 tablespoons golden or maple syrup	3–4 tablespoons maple syrup
2 oz (55g) walnuts	½ cup walnuts

1. Put the crumbs in a bowl. Drain and mash the tofu and add to the crumbs. Stir in the spices.

2. Add just enough syrup to make the mixture hold together without being too sticky. Mix well.

3. Divide the mixture and shape each piece into a small ball.

4. Coarsely crush the walnuts and roll the balls in them, making sure each one is thickly and evenly coated. Arrange on a plate or tray and chill well before serving.

INDEX

157

Of further interest . . .

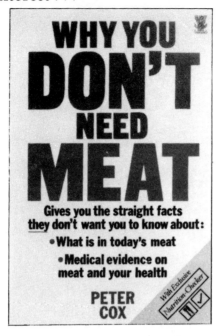

WHY YOU DON'T NEED MEAT

Peter Cox. There is mounting scientific proof that the meat we eat today actually *causes* heart disease, cancer, obesity and other degenerative diseases. The author exposes the black market in animal growth hormones, looks at the unregulated use of antibiotics in animal feed and shows why a meat orientated diet can actually be nutritionally deficient.

The Classic Vegan Cookbook
Co-published with the Vegan Society

EVA BATT'S VEGAN COOKERY

A completely revised and updated edition of Eva Batt's WHAT'S COOKING? which has become accepted as the classic work on vegan cookery. Now this invaluable book is relaunched retaining all the help, advice and information for which it is well-known but with a new, clear presentation and layout, metric and imperial measures, and up-to-date product information, making it of even more value to vegan cooks, novice and experienced everywhere.

As a vegan of nearly thirty years standing, the name of Eva Batt is, for many, synonmous with vegan cookery. Her work on ensuring that a diet can be healthily balanced, as well as both enjoyable and compassionate, has been extensive and scientific. The result is a breadth of knowledge second-to-none, a range of carefully planned and tested recipes for all occasions, and thus a handbook which will be welcomed by everyone interested in a way of life which brings both health and peace of mind.